Keith W

IRRITABLE VOW   ROME

First Published 2011 by Appin Press, an imprint of Countyvise Ltd
14 Appin Road, Birkenhead, CH41 9HH

British Library Cataloguing in Publication Data.A catalogue record for this book is available from the British Library.

ISBN 978 1 906205 75 1

Contents

Foreword

Like my Dad, Mr Wilson has a great love of words AND their manipulation - and like all Liverpudlians, it's IMPOSSIBLE to keep the humour out. Even when he's being serious, it's always bubbling under like a volcano waiting to erupt. It's the curse of all of us Scousers - but come to think of it, not such a bad ailment (unless it erupts from a serious newsreader's trousers during a live TV news bulletin - and I've just seen that happen!) WHY try to suppress humour? (You kan't kan you keith?) If humour were suppressed we'd all go round with squashed smiles .... you might as well be outrageous like our Keith. The book title says it all - *Irritable Vowel Syndrome* - with lines like *'borderline obscene, but never heard'* .... *'he can flog all his weaknesses dressed up as strength'* .... *'accepting Tweets from complete and utter strangers'* ....
and in the poem 'Derby Day,' the charming *'pretend you're content with a draw'.*

Obviously, trying to survive in today's uncertain world has its many painful pitfalls. But let's be honest - when it comes right down to it, LIFE'S A LAF. At least, thank God, in Keith's world it is.

Mike McCartney

Irritable Vowel Syndrome

It's not a book of poetry
But a book with poetry in
A travel-lodge-travelogue-soapy-doc-opera
That starts as it means to begin
About people and things
Lots and not much
Two-footed tackles
And the deftest of touch
High protein, low fat roadside snack bars
Economy class air travel and boys' smells in cars

Liniment, 'leccy guitars
Sheep and despair
Issy Myake
And Ferrero Rocher
Time and decay
Light and shade
Those who've really got it
And those who've got it made
On a highbrow, lowbrow
Disposable and permanent
Cheap day return
Between the gutter
And the firmament
By a fraudulent weaver
Of linguistic spells
Who writes in bruises
And anonymous hotels
Delivering big words
With a neat line and length
So he can flog all his weaknesses
Dressed up as strength
In tales of modern hardware
And tough, urban life

Of gods and gobshites
And the world and his wife
Flatulence, depression
Spring onions, Pink Floyd
The kissed off, the pissed off
And the slightly annoyed

There's places, faces
And flat-packed grounds
Shekels and Euros
Monopoly dosh and Pounds
Big balls and little balls
Racquets, studs and bats
Feigning reigning champions
And raining dogs and cats
Ear wax and haemorrhoids
The scally millionaire
Elvis sideburns, bum fluff
Own goals and nose fur
Flavours of the month
Flagging up the latest saviour
The link between poor diet
And outrageous behaviour
European one-night stands
And continental drift
And the vocational epiphany
When everyone got epiphed

Think of a low budget version
Of Gulliver's Travels (without the bondage)
That occasionally twists
Turns and unravels
More Houyhnhnm than Yahoo
More Nerys Hughes than Ted
A veritable dog's dinner
On a piece of wholemeal bread

Where paragraphs wait to be sentenced
And commas slip into comas
A healthy slice of life's warp and weft
With name-dropping misnomers
All wrapped up in a book of bits
Or even a bit of a book
An heir apparent amongst the remaindered section
That nobody bothered to pick up

Overlooking the gratuitous
Labyrinthine prose
The shin splints, the broken hearts
And the cauliflower nose
I'm sure it's got a format
I'm just not sure what it is
But it's well hard for a softback
And it's sorted for cheese and whizz

So if it's beauty you're after, with romance
And perhaps a clever twist
Read it Saturday night, half eleven
Curried-up and pissed

Manifesto

To make the world a far better place
We'd breakfast on strawberry Cornetto
And a Practical Utopianism weekly supplement
Would come free with the Liverpool Echo

Progressive thinking would stretch the unflexible
With thoughts made from knicker elastic
Hotel keys would look and feel like keys
Not dysfunctional pieces of plastic

Wikipedia would be factually correct
Potential partner's baggage regularly checked
No more ringing tills for that dark, satanic Heather Mills
And there'd be Smarties on the NHS to cure all ills

Primary schools would teach a love of jazz and blues
Dancing would be compulsory in all bus queues
Marmite soldiers would be the peace-keeping force
And every jockey would ride a gift-horse

Wannabe WAG's would refrain from kissing frogs
Non-patrons encouraged to use public house bogs
There'd be loads more kissing but no kiss and tell
And free optimism available in a handy gel

There'd be space hopper taxis for fake fur trappers
Complimentary wrapping paper for prankster rappers
Free megaphones for those unheard voices
And a legal right to work with multiple choices

There'd be monthly cash prizes for freestyle sneezing
No more pain and suffering in the football season
Street fights replaced by pavement debates
And all weather bulletins sung by Tom Waits

Free school milk for the under sixteens
Kelvin McKenzie blown to smithereens
Giant-sized Connect 4 in every town centre
And private health care for sufferers of kids' TV presenter

Bubble wrap as currency and pocket-size stress relief
A rambler's right to roam and a gurner's right to teeth
And a recommended daily intake of high jinks and low fat
With Laurel and Hardy, Catweazle, The Flintstones and Top Cat

There'd be counselling for every Bluetooth earpiece wearer
At least an O.B.E. for every voluntary carer
Town Hall politics would be clean as a whistle
With no more clown tribunals for Fun Fair dismissal
Happy hour would last all day, stress-free and enjoyable
All Traffic Wardens would be forever unemployable
There'd be no internet connection for Leslie Grantham
And 'Give Peace A Chance' would be the new national anthem

What a wonderful world it could be …….

Bloodline

For Thomas James Wilson

Much have I travelled - and much have I seen
I have absorbed and inhaled laughter lines and forward lines
Drawn battle lines across time lines
And followed lay lines through good times and bad

It gets under the skin
It leaves its mark
And is worn with pride

Five stars flicker in the firmament, burn the memory
and warm a deep and unconditional love
that serves to remind us
that all we need
is each other

Afterthought

I had a thought today
Just the one - I'm not greedy

I listened to the look of it
And I looked at the sound of it
I picked it up and shook it
Bounced it off the ground a bit
I walked around the back of it
Talked behind its back a bit
Opened the window and let it loose
And couldn't keep track of it
I started to shout a bit
Kicked it about a bit
Put it in my pocket
And then went out with it
Walked the walk with it
Talked the talk with it
Opened up a can of worms
With a knife and fork with it

Keeping it real with it
I shook on a deal with it
Run it past myself again
And went out for a meal with it
Had too much to drink with it
Threw up in the sink with it
Tried to recall the cause of it all
Until I couldn't think with it

I think I had a thought today
I thought it worth a mention
But I'll think again on second thoughts
I think it's nervous tension

Moan Sweet Moan

Without the ability to moan
Straight jackets would be the national costume
Available on the High Street in a range of fashionable colours

Without the ability to moan
Street cleaners would seriously clean up
As people hurled themselves from an inconvenient height

Without the ability to moan
Thousands of people would die of frustration
Trapped inside complex and ineffective complaints procedures

Without the ability to moan
Artists would draw nothing but blood
Illustrated by inflamed irritation and colourful language

Without the ability to moan
Saga holidays would collapse as would-be sun seekers
Spent their money on cider and hung around shopping precincts

Without the ability to moan
The NHS would crumble and fall into a sea
Of strokes, heart attacks and daily suicide attempts

Moaning is good for you
It relaxes self-control
It's therapeutic, clears the air
Cleanses the soul
Releases pent-up tension
Allows the mind to breathe
And the heart shows its true colours
On the snotty end of your sleeve
Isn't this Government rubbish?
I hate Traffic Wardens, don't you?
Have you tried to get a plumber out on Saturday night?

Or seen a Post Office without a queue?

What happened to indicating at roundabouts?
And what's going on with the weather?
Do cyclists think they're motorists or pedestrians?
And that stuff's plastic – not faux leather!

Why are people doing 50 in the outside lane?
The whole country's going to the dogs
Let's bring back hanging for queue jumpers
And for God's sake, let's bring back public bogs

Reformed smokers - what a pain in the arse
And what's that Scientology all about?
I'm sick of looking for the end of the sellotape
And why do parcels always turn up when you're out?

Why can't you shoot to kill a tailgating white van man?
Why no crossbow application for your phone?
Why do wasps insist on being so anti-social?
And how do Jehovah's Witnesses know when you're home?

Moaning is good for you
It relaxes self-control
It's therapeutic, clears the air
Cleanses the soul
Releases pent-up tension
Allows the mind to breathe
And the heart shows its true colours
On the snotty end of your sleeve

It could be bottled water
Or debt consolidation
Junk mail, pollution
The state of the nation
Screaming kids, traffic
Celebrity, late trains

Shrink-wrapped CD's
Varicose veins
Mosquitos, television
Or those annoying ringtones
Whatever it is that gets your goat
We all love a good moan

Without the ability to moan
All football phone-ins would fall silent
And fans everywhere would lose the ability to speak

Without the ability to moan
Women would adopt semaphore signals
So that blokes would know exactly when to take out the bins

Without the ability to moan
There would be nothing
Only chaos

All Loved Up

A contemporary dose of the unrequiteds in the key of F off sharp

You never, ever write and you never, ever phone
But once there was a time you couldn't leave me alone
It was almost as if we joined at the hip
With super glue and double-sided tape
It was all racing pulses and languid limbs
Delicious absurdities and pseudonyms
It was all warm and curious by my inside pocket
You'd melted my aorta

Why did you do those things
The way you did, the way I tried?
There's nothing I could say, nothing I could do
If only you'd talked about it
Instead of waiting, hesitating
I could've been all loved up with you

I realised I loved you when it didn't bother me
When you eat your Chicken Balti off my Hawkwind LP
And I let you wipe your nose on my favourite sleeve
Which was 'Sticky Fingers' by the Stones
I suppose I should've known it was too good to be true
But you know what it was like when I stood in front of you
I was besotted by your ears, nose and throat
In fact I loved your bones

Why did you do those things
The way you did, the way I tried?
There's nothing I could say, nothing I could do
If only you'd talked about it
Instead of waiting, hesitating
I could've been all loved up with you

But all of a sudden our lovin' cup
Shattered, runneth over and went tits up
I didn't know whether to draw a line
Line a drawer or have a liquorice allsort
But I miss you more now
Than I missed you then
And when your karma kills your dogma
Says the little book of Zen
If your heart had a heart to heart
You know it wouldn't lie

Why did you do those things
The way you did, the way I tried?
There's nothing I could say, nothing I could do
If only you'd talked about it

Instead of waiting, hesitating
I could've been all loved up with you

Progressively Worse

I've been losing my looks since I was eleven
My six pack's now a Watneys Party Seven
And I'm eyeing a Stannah Stairway to Heaven
Things are getting progressively worse

I look like I've been fast-tracked for management at Greggs
I'm in fear of constipation through a love of boiled eggs
Even my best trousers are on their last legs
Things are getting progressively worse

I went out with a girl who didn't mind she didn't matter
She was about as interesting a haddock in batter
Never said a word - even her teeth didn't chatter
Things are getting progressively worse

I have the dreams from which stuff is made
I smoke chocolate cigarettes while dizzy on lemonade
At the merest hint of Virginia Woolf I'm more than afraid
Things are getting progressively worse

There's a shrinkage problem with most of my clothes
I'm developing a fondness for West End shows
I've got a full head of hair growing out of my nose
Things are getting progressively worse

I got stung by a wasp on the upper inner thigh
I kissed Georgie Porgie's sister and made myself cry
I rang the Samaritans and got no reply
Things are getting progressively worse

I've stopped listening to Camel, Gong and Caravan
Soft Machine, Henry Cow, King Crimson and Can
Van der Graaf Generator, Faust and Man
Things are getting progressively worse

I can't remember things I thought I'd never forget
I suffer flashbacks of an ex-girlfriend called Bernadette
She was psychic and left me three weeks before we met
Things are getting progressively worse

Non-Traditionally Beautiful

*A cautionary tale of cosmetic enhancement straight from the
horse's lips*

Things were sweet when he first held her hand
That week in Rhyl in his mum's caravan
All potato wedged up with sour cream
Sharing salt and vinegar Pringles with love's young dream
But caught in the half light
He was nutted by despair
She came back from the laundrette with her flaws laid bare

She told him she loved him but she didn't like her ears
The size of her nose had reduced her to tears
She had tram lines on both of her eyes
And struggled finding leggings that could handle her thighs
And through conjunctivitis
He could see that her pain was real
So they talked about it over coffee and a Wagon Wheel

In the blink of an eye she'd had an eye brow lift
Bought a pair of those tits a JCB couldn't shift
A collagen trout-pout and a botoxed head
And was looking like an extra from 'Shaun of the Dead'
Before he could say Pot Noodle
She was under the knife to augment
Those well-worn weather-beaten flaps on the front of her tent

Spider veins, crow's feet
Liposuction, reet petite
Face lifts, perma-tans
Easy term payment plans

She was non-traditionally beautiful
And he loved her just as she was
White lines, tummy tucks, buttocks and thighs
Belly button sculpture, non-reflective eyes
Sphincter realignment to lift it off the deck
And a bag-head's pony tail to sort the turkey neck
And through what looked like a road kill
As he watched her new ears being pinned
He saw that she now had a face like a cat breaking wind

So love yourself, love your skin
Love your body and all within

Ad infinitum, add paint, add jam
Ad lib, add water, ad nauseam

Take one corset, eat as many cakes as you can
And spill forth ....

Hare Krishna
Harry Windsor
Harry Redknapp
Harry Ramsden

Meet Me On The Corner

Meet me on the corner
Well not exactly on the corner
Around the corner from the corner
Past the bus stop
I'm not one for grand gestures
More token gestures
Hence the card and gift voucher
For the pet shop
But there's things I need to say
Things you need to hear
Things I've got to get
Off my chest
I know about you and him
Dancing skin to skin
So if we meet out in the street
It's probably best

I'll be discreet when we meet
And greet in the street
And I'll be dressed
In my best behaviour
There'll be hardly any mention
Of the underlying tension
And I certainly won't use
The 'F' word – Failure
That could be evocative,
Insensitive, provocative
And I really wouldn't want
To make things worse
Unless this really is the end
And we're all done and dusted
In which case
I'll retaliate first

If you fail to prepare
You prepare to fail
So here's one
I prepared earlier
You say he's taller
And better looking than me
But I'll bet he's never
Given you a hernia

I told myself I wouldn't
And I shouldn't but if I can't
Keep a lid on all the things I want to say
It's just the way it is
The way I am, the way it goes
That stiff upper lip thing's so passé
So he plays the trombone
And he makes you laugh
And he's an erudite arty farty
Well, trombones were invented
By some drunken plumber
In the bog at a pipe fitter's party

How can you take this man seriously?
He's hardly at the sharp end of cool
He may be an educated man of letters
But there's still only one 'f' in fool

Remember *Love Me Do*
On the king-size kazoo
That night you bent down
And bared your soul?
When you told me that you
Struggled with intimacy
And I told you
I was crap in goal
That's the kind of love
That money just can't buy

Something powerful and strong
You can't forget
Like the lingering stench
Of this new bloke's after shave
That smelt like a badger
With a stomach upset

I bet he even speaks in predictive text
And his breath smells like the arse of Hades
Surely no man's made a greater effort on his own behalf
To stun and repel the ladies

Now me and you are through
It's up to you what you do
You've proved there's no accounting for taste
But I can't help thinking
When I look into the mirror
Jesus Christ – what a waste

So let's not meet on the corner
Well not exactly on the corner
Around the corner from the corner
Past the bus stop
I've got loads of stuff to do
I've got to go to B & Q
There's two drains
And the sink to unblock
I'll get over the sorrow
By midday tomorrow
And although there'll never be another you
I look forward to the day
When the chance comes to repay
That tromboning bastard's IOU

Sensitive Eddie

After months of protracted fight negotiations,
it finally came to a head. The gloves were off,
the verbal exchanges had degenerated nicely
and a date had been written into the diary in

blue black ink. For the neutral, this was a tough
one to call, as neither contender looked likely to
kiss the canvas. They knew each other well –
height, weight, trademark punch – and there was

nothing between them. Throughout the course of
the pre-fight scuffles, during which time a snooker
table was flattened, two hotel waiters knocked out
and the gusset violently ripped out of an occupied

pair of Speedos, it became clear that both fighters
were more than up for the challenge – and both
were capable of inflicting serious damage. Hooks,
straight rights, lefts, uppercuts, jabs, head butts, flash

knockdowns, the low blow and the odd rabbit punch
had all been used to good effect in previous encounters.
If this was to go the distance, the corner men would have
to use all their tactical nous and experience to find a

winning combination. This would be a street fight. A brawl.
Pride, self-respect and reputations were at stake – and some
serious money was riding on the outcome. Seconds out and
they set about each other - straight from the first bell ....

        Blood and snot
        skin and hair
        tooth and nail
        him and her

with uncontrolled aggression
no Queensbury Rules
no cauliflower 'earsay
no selling out to fools
no golden handshakes
no unloaded gloves
no comedy of errors
no loss of love
no pulling of punches
no shattering glass jaws
no dropping the guard
no hitting the floor
no ducking and diving
no cheek by jowl
no talk of surrender
no throwing in the towel …….

With eyes so bloodied
they could hardly see
and lips too swollen to speak
fighting talk bleeds
into legal small talk and
what it's worth inherits the meek
along with the house, the car and the kids
removed without anaesthetic or remorse
file your nails, your bankruptcy, file your own teeth
before you think about filing for divorce
without speaking to the best at this difficult time
pick up our free, handbag-friendly CD Rom
and for all of your get-rid-quick divorce requirements
call Sensitive Eddie now at binbag.com

Blind Date

We met by the mouth wash in Poundland
My internet blind date and me
I wasn't tall, dark and handsome
And she wasn't twenty three

I half-attempted to crack a smile
But instead, cracked a head gasket
Wishing she'd disappear into the ether
Like Chicken in the Basket

I said not much and she said less
In fluent, monosyllabic stutter
You could've cut the atmosphere
With a special atmosphere cutter

So I grabbed a bag of figs and a Toilet Duck
And five quid's worth of crisps from the aisles
Nutted the security guard, legged it from the shop
And kept on running for forty seven miles

Moonlight

Moonlight becomes you
It goes with your facial hair
Your asymmetric grimace
And disconcerting stare

Your pointed ears and hairy palms
Size twelve hobnailed feet
Those bushy, slanted eyebrows
And that lust for raw sausage meat

The fallout from your flatulence
In itself would be grounds for divorce
The noise alone would wake the dead
The stench would stun a horse

But it's the mood swings and the howling
The foul language under your breath
It's like cutting carrots with the Grim Reaper
I feel like I'm dicing with death

Caught between a frock and a hard place
Every month for at least seven days
It's like standing on a plank between two ladders
While reality comes in and out of phase

Walking and talking on eggshells
All diluted cordiality forsaken
I'm left in no doubt it's called PMT because
Mad Cow Disease was already taken

She Said I Was A Dreamer

She said I was a dreamer
That I wouldn't amount to much
That I lived in some kind of parallel world
And lacked the Midas touch
I was shallow and avoided reality
But it doesn't really matter now
She won the lottery and lives Spain
The bleedin' lucky cow

MF

There's something tapping on the window pane
Something in the air outside the door
You can sense its scent under the floorboards
Feel it's breath at your body's core
It carries the carrion of yesterday's you
In a moist paper handkerchief
It lurks in the shadows and bides its time
And is loaded with serious grief

And then all of a sudden and suddenly
From the darkness at dead of night
You're attacked with military precision
As it kicks seven shades of shite
Out of the XY chromosome carrier
It's a scientific fact – sad but true
And now only prayers can save the forsaken life
Of a victim of Man-Flu

Fever, runny nose, dry cough, sore throat
Severe muscle aches and the shivers
Diarrhea smoothies with every cough
And flatulence that always delivers
Stomach cramps, tight chest
That chronic pain in your back
Blowing snot bubbles when you force a laugh
And sweating like a glass blowers' crack

But you never throw in the towel
When the crap hits the pan
You take it on the chin
You take it like a man

Obviously you're desperate
To drag yourself into work
Despite the serious health risks involved
But as a man you're far too selfless
To risk spreading the disease
So you stay off with Jeremy Kyle – problem solved

But you must let everybody know
How completely shit you feel
And it's crucial that you tell other men
So they can prepare themselves mentally
Clear the couch and fill the fridge
Should this horrendous potential killer attack them

Never strain for the remote, always keep it to hand
With your iPod, phone, newspaper and pen
And absorb those NHS pamphlets
GQ, Men's Health and FHM
Despite the pain you should never forget
You're an expert in self-diagnosis
And never be influenced by the female persuasion
They're prone to bouts of psychosis

Men don't moan with Man-Flu
They hold the agony within
Maybe there's the occasional sigh
In proportion to the pain they're in
But that's just a lovely way to involve a partner
And suggest it would really be sweet
If she dabbed your head with a moistened sponge
And maybe gently massaged your feet

You must resist those effeminate 'lady medicines'
You know the ones they always keep 'just in case'
All that stuff off the shelf's for the common cold
For MF that's beyond an insult - it's a disgrace

This is more painful than childbirth
It attacks only the strongest physiques
And childbirth's all over in a few hours
Man-Flu lasts for weeks

Fever, runny nose, dry cough, sore throat
Severe muscle aches and the shivers
Diarrhea smoothies with every cough
And flatulence that always delivers
Stomach cramps, chest pains
That chronic pain in your back
Blowing snot bubbles when you force a laugh
And sweating like a glass blowers' crack

But you never throw in the towel
When the crap hits the pan
You take it on the chin
Because you're a man

And while there's still no cure
For the common cold
Your man's man can soothe the disease
With Night Nurse, Pot Noodles
Match of the Day and brandy
And a prescription of Russ Meyer DVD's

Bag Peace

There are those who've probably got bags of time
And those with bags of space
Those with bags of the folding stuff
Who've bagged the best seats in the place
Those with bags of energy
And those with bags to spare
Those who let the cat out of the bag
And those without a bag who don't care

Bags guaranteed to keep your salad moist
And bags to keep your perishables fresh
Those who need bags of encouragement
And bags to bring the mobile crèche
Those with kitbags packed with troubles
Jangling bags carrying bottles of bubbles
Handbags and gladrags that really look the biz
And dried-up bags that've lost a bit of fizz

Bags that exceed the permitted inch rate
Bags that get up early but are always late
Bags that drag you down 'cos their handles are bust
Scallywags with scally bags in search of upper crust
Bags of rules and bags of regs
Bags full of quality and bags full of dregs
Bags that take an inch and bags that take a mile
Bags full of cunning and bags full of guile
Bags for bagging off and bags for clocking on
Bags that are missing and bags that've gone
Bags of experience and bags of charm
Bags on the dance floor and bags on the arm
Sleeping bags and sick bags hand in hand
Battered leather flight bags permanently tanned
School bags and duffle bags packed by mother
Sainsbury's and Tesco bags snarling at each other

Man bags and travel bags jockey for position
Bin bags and bean bags and bags on a mission
Bags full of this and bags full of that
Bags full of quality and bags full of tat
Saddle bags and air bags in all their glory
Money bags on jazz fags inevitably Tory
Banging on and bagging off in paper boys' bags
And bags full of plastic modelled by WAGS

Bags on the shoulder, bags under the eyes
Vinegar-soaked bags teasing soggy fries
Crisp bags and lucky bags dying to be kissed
All night party bags permanently pissed
Messenger bags laden with lies
Grease-proof bags hugging steak and kidney pies
Laptop bags that sit on your knee
Over-ripe fun bags silicone-free
Paper bags, plazzy bags, doggy bag chic
Bags on the wind playing hide and seek
J. Edgar Hoover bags of white line wheezes
And carrier bags for designer diseases

Bags of sweets with bags of class
Bags of front carrying bags of grass
Goody bags and shoulder bags looking for a ride
Overnight re-useable bags fitted and supplied

There are those who've probably got bags of time
And those with bags of space
Those with bags of the folding stuff
Who've bagged the best seats in the place
Those with bags of energy
And those with bags to spare
But the one to swerve is the body bag
There's no fake Louis Vuitton there

Lover

I love her sense of humour
I love her bright blue eyes
Her sense of fun and peachy bum
Her little white lies

I love the way she bites her lip
The way she holds her head
I love her party buffets
She does a lovely spread

I love the way she listens
I love her underwear
I love the fact her ego
Isn't bigger than her hair

I love her parking sensors
When she pulls up to my bumper
I love her little pixie nose
And I love her lumpy jumper

I love her winsome, windswept look
When her hair blows in the breeze
I love her post modern topiary
A foot above her knees

I love the way she looks at me
With that twinkle in her eye
After I've been out jogging
And had a Mars Bar on the sly

I love her in the morning
I love her late at night
I love it when we argue
I love a decent fight

I love her inner strength
I love the smell of her hair
I love her over here
I love her over there

I love her sixties hippy look
All Westwood, bangles and belts
I love the fact that she's unique
Just like everyone else

I love her two-egg omelette
Sprawled across her plate
But I don't love her half as much
As I love her flat mate

More Balls Than Most

From pit boots to slingbacks without passing go

Sometimes I'll notice you
And sometimes I won't
Sometimes you fascinate
And sometimes you don't
With Max Factor eyes
That look out of their heads
And a gob that strangles vowels
While they sleep in their beds
You look manly and awkward
And your clothes are second-hand
A sort of buy one and get one free
One night stand
Like Bette Davis in 'Baby Jane'
The resemblance is uncanny
But most of us have lay in bed
With an ear cocked to a tranny

You've been around the block a bit
And to be honest it shows
But I'm intrigued by a face
That's sixty five per cent nose
With a lorry driver's jacksy
Wrapped in glad rags
You gargle pints of wife beater
And smoke diet fags
Walking someone else's walk
And dressing very up
And stuffing those chicken fillet things
In a double D cup
Loving bri-nylon
Chapter and verse
But you're long ways parked dear
In a sideways universe

Dressing up, dressing down
You love Ethel Austin
Big hands, little hands
Like Rosemary in thyme
Dressing up, dressing down
You love Ethel Austin
But you've got more balls than most
Hidden up your sleeve

I've seen your best moves
On the bacon counter
A latter day L-o-l-a
In a modern briefs encounter
Dressing like your mother dressed
In 1966
And taking it on a stubbled chin
From stones and sticks
Trapped inside those corduroy kecks
For all those years
You were sucked through a man-hole
By a flash flood of tears
Give it to me straight
And tell me why
In a big girl's blouse
Big boys don't cry

In polyester slacks
From the sale at T.K.Maxx
And a bra from the Army and Navy
You've permed your legs
And waxed your hair
And now there's no lumps in your gravy
You told your ex-wife
That you'd changed your life
And you wrote in a note that you missed her
Then for old time's sake

You ran your big, hairy hands
Up and down her sister

Dressing up, dressing down
You love Ethel Austin
Big hands, little hands
Like Rosemary in thyme
Dressing up, dressing down
You love Ethel Austin
But you've got more balls than most
Hidden up your sleeve

Cushion Talk

Dry mouth, blurred vision
Constipation, indecision
I'm all at sea in an ocean of commotion
Expectation, inflammation
Agitation, perspiration
Even my pants are crackling with static emotion

You're playing with my heart again
After promising so much
And those catalogue diamond ring tones
That we swapped to keep in touch
Only serve to remind me
As we near the final curves
You're living in another world
And I'm on pills for my nerves

Thrilling fields or killing fields
Which one will it be?
You've got all the answers
'cos I know it isn't me
That's sitting in the driving seat
Crashing through the gears
And now you've managed to park your arse
It'll probably all end in tears

It's not my fault
I'm not keen on holding hands
Or that every time your mum comes round
She misunderstands
A sophisticated sense of humour
Considers me impolite
Takes off her sovereign rings
And insists that we fight

Heartbreaks and heartaches
May strengthen the spine
But this is about you and me now
So I might as well speak my mind

I can't stand the candles
That you burn around the bath
Or the thirty thousand cushions
That you've scattered round the gaff
That you're a vegetarian
And I am what I eat
If God didn't want us to eat animals
Why make them out of meat?

I hate your damp washing
On my exercise bike
The fact you won't buy bacon
Or those full fat crisps I like
Your migraines, mood swings
The fairground for the cat
And your constant interference
With the heating thermostat

You tidy up my stuff
And I never see it again
I don't know where
Don't know when
And you re-arrange house and home
According to feng shui
And I've got to put the bog seat down
Just like the mystics say

But then again ....

You have got lovely eyes
Especially the one on the right
I'd probably miss your nut roasts
Every other Friday night
I'd miss your whistling nostrils
When you doze in front of the box
Your pencil moustache and your flatulence
After the cabbage soup detox

You're playing with my heart again
After promising so much
And those extended forked tongues
That we swapped to keep in touch
Only serve to remind me
That it pays to think things through
So I'll say what I mean and mean what I say
I just won't say them to you

Aerosol

I'm neither happy nor impressed with my aerosol
Or the 24 hour protection claim it makes
I sprayed armpit and thigh to keep me fresh and dry
And half a quid isn't cheap for God's sake
But I was wired and perspired to burn out it transpired
My nether regions felt like they were being kiln fired
Sweet essence of gorilla could be smelt from afar
I was sweating like a gerbil in a Turkish gay bar

I'd followed the serving suggestions to the letter
Shook the can, removed the lid and took aim
Applied a thin film of industrial-smelling aerosol dry ice
And an aspirin chaser to numb the pain
With calamine lotion to cool the irritation
And half a bottle of gin to soothe the nerves
Two pickled gherkins for the sandpaper rash
In a poultice of kumquat preserve
Because the last time I used it I felt terrible
Although it could've been the six pints of Draught Bass
Disagreeing with the home brew Bavarian bitter
The two Lamb Bhunas and Chicken Madras
But on reflection it's more likely an aerosol reaction
I mean, do we really know what's in this stuff?
Have you seen what it does to the armpits on your shirts?
And when it soils your undergarments enough's enough

It's not just the environment that CFC's attack
I could be damaging the boyzone layer
Imagine subjecting your prize-winning spuds
To a pesticide-loaded crop sprayer

It's much better to smell like a real man
Aromatherapy wasn't built in a day
So I'll splash myself all over with bread crumb aftershave
It doesn't half attract the birds I've got to say
So I'm saying this and I'm sticking to it
And take heed to avoid any sorrow
No more aerosols after today
Roll-on tomorrow

Twitter Ye Not

It's come to something when conversation
Floats face down in the water
And talking with your mouth is reduced to its knees
Attention span to the slaughter
Whatever happened to the gift of the gob
The natter, the patter and the chatter
Throwing the lips into forming words
And fiddling with the old grey matter

I want to talk to you in real time
While you're there, face to face throughout
But all this Facebook, Myspace, Bebo, Flickr, Twitter stuff's
Completely freaking me out
All I've had is a poke on your wall
And some static interference from Al Jaziera
I've been under the doctor for the last eighteen months
Craving for the analogue era

What have I got to do to get through to you?
All I want is a quick word
You spend more time with your phone on the blog
Borderline obscene but never heard
Sending me texts saying you've left a message
Behind the wall on your Facebook page
I can't get a word in now your new best mates
Are talking absolute bollocks centre stage

Hundreds of friends you've never even met
Dissecting what Katy drank next
Brown-nosed browsers kissing each others' trousers
Immersed in the joy of text

OMG! I did the best toilet ever!
I had a whole coffee cake with my tea!

I laughed so much I sucked my trousers up my arse
And the cartilage popped out of my knee! LOL!

And Tristram died in a blogging accident
The poor unfortunate soul

He was poked by a stoker from Kuala Lumpur
And couldn't find the blog roll

Fifi's done a runner and left me with the kids
Kylie, Ptolemy and Chlamydia

Twatted me on Twitter, all twisted and bitter
Said 'I couldn't friggin' wait to get rid of yer'
And who could forget y'know, whats' her name?
Her with the three million friends
Found in bed with an inflatable sheep
And friction burns at both ends …….

But I say this
With some confidence
Peppered with two fingers of wit
For the most part
All of this Twitterati stuff
Should be filed under 'Who Gives A Shit?'

I won't even mention
The potential dangers
Of accepting Tweets
From complete and utter strangers

So unplug your iPod, laptop and mobile
And let's gaze into each others' eyes
We can swap words and sentences made with conversation
It's the coolest way to tell each other lies

This impersonal stuff can make the heart grow harder
Aggressive, mean-spirited, even nasty
And we both know nothing electronic can say 'I love you'
More than a bunch of forecourt flowers and a Ginster's pasty

It's come to something when conversation
Floats face down in the water
And talking with your mouth is reduced to its knees
Attention span to the slaughter
Whatever happened to the gift of the gob
The natter, the patter and the chatter
Throwing the lips into forming words
And fiddling with the old grey matter

I wanted to talk to you in real time
While you were there, face to face throughout
But all this Facebook, Myspace, Bebo, Flickr, Twitter stuff's
Completely freaked me out

I'm not interested in tweeting or poking
And now the will to live has almost diminished
I've texted you to say
I've been on ebay
And bought a Thai bride
Sod off - we're finished

Lie Back And Think of England

Biggles
Red phone boxes
Isombard Kingdom Brunel
Punch and Judy
Village greens
Ronco and K-Tel

T.S. Eliot
Vivian Stanshall
Motorway Service Stations
Stonehenge
Morris dancing
Sausage, egg and bacon

Bulldog spirit
London buses
Home-made traffic jam
Ambivalence
The River Thames
A peculiar fondness for Spam

Jellied eels
Wagon Wheels
English as a second language
Buckingham Palace
The cricket bat
Black pudding on a sandwich

Grammar Schools
Rural Shires
Pride before a fall
Winston Churchill
The Beatles
Canon and Ball

Wimbledon
Blackpool Rock
The White Cliffs of Dover
Bowler hats
Tea towels
Dogs called Rover

James Bond
Suet pudding
Rupert the Bear
Glastonbury
Oxbridge
The rip-off train fare

Travel rugs
Harry Potter
Never saying sorry
Big Ben
News at Ten
Stuff off the back of a lorry

Syd Barrett
Fish and Chips
The Army and Navy Stores
Shakespeare
The Archers
Fur coats and no drawers

Dennis Potter
Merseybeat
The Angel of the North
Brian Sewell
Real ale
Tony Hart and Morph

Wilfred Owen
Billy Bragg
Stiff Upper Lip
Perpetual queuing
The Two Ronnies
Legs that give you jip

Tracey Emin
Poundland
Pork scratchings and darts
Benny Hill
The Magic Roundabout
Grown men lighting farts

Villagers
And pillagers
Chaps called Carruthers
Sunlight Soap
Tea-strainers
Knitted bog roll covers

Brighton Pier
Marmite
Dunlop Green Flash
Royal Ascot
Barbara Windsor
Schoolkids on the lash

The Panto Dame
Sarcasm
Betty's Tea Rooms
Hot-dog stands
Curtain twitching
Silver coke spoons

Bargain hunting
Candy floss
Political correctness
The Women's Institute
Pearly Kings
A lack of all directness

Marks and Sparks
Roast beef
Eccentrics and slackers
Moaning and groaning
Potted Meat
Bri-nylon undercrackers

George Formby
Yorkshire pud
The BBC
Insularity
Socks with sandals
And endless cups of tea

Kensington Fields Forever

Back then
The streets weren't paved with gold
But somehow sparkled with an authentic glint

Back then
The world was full of holes
But that was where the light got in

Back then
The sky would smile and whisper
As if secrets were being told to friends

Back then
Turns twisted and twists returned
En route to journey's end

      Now those half-remembered dreams
      Ragged at the seams
      Flicker in black and white
      On subconscious screens
      And are thrown and blown
      To smithereens by the thought
      Of the way we were

Playing on the debris
Fred Flintstone
Plastic sandals
The Hippodrome

The Man From Uncle
Wayfinder shoes
The Rag and Bone Man
Reds and Blues

The Zephyr 6
The Ford Cortina
Troy Tempest
Aqua Marina

Play Streets
Action Man
Capaldi's Café
Desperate Dan

Scott Tracy
Thunderbird 1
Alan Ball
Ian St. John

Sugar butties
Empire Day
Jack Sharp's
Stingray

Ice-lolly sticks
In sun-kissed tar
The Johnny Seven
My first guitar

      But now we're estranged
      I barely recognise your face
      My heart beats another skip
      And thinks without a trace
      Whatever happened to you and me
      Jayne Hewitt and Karen Bentley
      Jimmy Williams and Tommy Quinn
      And the Kensington they wrapped us in

Butler Street School
Kenny Park
Joe, Paul
Steve and Mark

Ivy's shop
Proper Scouse
Green cream soda
The Wash House

Mrs. Ravenscroft
Mummy Noone
Stanley Hanson
A man on the Moon

Penny Arrow Bars
Crackerjack
Boaler Street Baths
Mars Attacks!

Bubble gum cards
Green Shield Stamps
The Topper, The Beezer
Cast iron street lamps

There's no sound of 'My Regeneration'
To stimulate the ears
No sign of an urban make-over
To defy the passing years
Only fading memories
Of you and of me
And how close
We used to be

You beautiful dreamer
You daydream believer
You eloquent blasphemer

Kensington Fields forever

About Face

It's about resilience
It's about strength
It's about character
It's about us
It's about them

Under fire or under focus, you justify, rationalise
You cover cracks in speech and body language
Ensure the strain will never show

It's about self belief
It's about this and that
Occasionally, it's about the other

It's about being bloody-minded and durable
It's about perseverance against the odds
It's about self-respect
It's about dignity

And it's about time we stood together
Strong, as one, shoulder to shoulder
And convinced women everywhere
That they too can take the bins out

Love Motion No.9

Should old acquaintance be forgot
And it has been a while now
Well, two weeks today to be precise
Since you bin-bagged me, you cow

I didn't mean to be dismissive or churlish
Or appear to be shallow and weak
I said those things with fingers crossed
Although my tongue was in someone else's cheek

I know that was well out of order
And I shouldn't have said your arms were fat
Or suggested your hundred quid haircut
Looked like a fire-damaged coconut mat

I'm sure you could've learned to love me
If you'd looked for the beauty within
I know you weren't keen on the double entendres
And I can't help slipping one in

But I'd rather remember the good times
Like that Tuesday when life was sweet
When we cemented our love on a futon
The Japanese word for concrete

So I've bought you something to remember me
It's not gold, diamonds or fake fur
It's a duffle coat made from real duffles
Wrapped in a pocket of air
It's not subdued but extravagant
In psychedelic tartan to turn heads
Three quarter length with rope loops
Bound in rare duffle hair threads

And once inside its warm silver-lined
Buttoned up embrace
The world and his wife and his dog 'Bastard'
Will seem a much warmer place

Although you're big boned, you're alright
And I know things can never be the same
I really am sorry for describing your face
Like a Picasso left out in the rain

So remember me through the duffle coat
Now you've chosen someone else instead
But if you're really going to stick with that haircut
Pull the hood up right over your head

You And Me

If you really love someone
That love will set them free
Like a bird from a cage
Like a cake from Dundee
But always let them know
You want them back in time for tea
I think that's where it all went wrong
For you and me

To The Spoon Of Tunerism

I'll never forget the day we mirst fet
Perfection from her tead to her hoes
She was singing and flicking powers
I was coughing and nicking my pose

She was into terbal hea and waiving the sails
And I was mostly into felling tibs
And because she was lush and chull-fested
I quite fancied dirst fibs

I told her I needed her like the rowers need the flain
Like a holo needs a pole
Like a beart needs a beartheat
And like Beetabix needs a wowl

As honesty is the pest of bolicies
There's never any loom for ries
So when she laid her tards on the cable
I told a complete lack of pies

We shared a brocolate chownie in Starbucks
With nine quid's worth of toffee and key
I wrote a popular tart chopper on the front of her shirt
Called 'Liver As Big As Hartlepool in 38D'

I'd been looking for love in every crook and nanny
And I was feeling like my flattery had gone bat
So I showed her my Post Orifice ravings account
And then, one night she let me coke her strat

She loved all things Foyal Ramily
Was forever dover-osing on caffeine
And randomly bursting into satriotic pong
'Sod Dave Our Spacious Queen'

What splendid fimes and tun we shared
Before she wore the second chouble din
I put on weight, wasn't looking grite as queat
And the pagpile sharpet had worn a bit thin

We soon began to bargue and icker
She'd shout and scream fight in my race
So to sort it all out, we played a cand of hards
For the the cog, the dat and the fantique ireplace

At the tard cable she threw down the who of tarts
I went with the spore of fades
She followed through with a clive of fubs
From up my sleeve I threw the space of aids
She hit me with the door of fireman's
I slapped down the whore of farts
Then she pulled a dive of fireman's with a clue of tubs
And I collapsed to the floor like a cack of pards

She punched the air and called me a smart feller
And laughed out loud bomping at the chit
But at least we parted on teaking sperms
And she'll remember me as a shining wit

Apocalipstick

When all about you
Are choosing their threads
And early bloomers are teased from their beds
All of another flutter a racing heart
Drags a comb through the air of expectancy

And the memory stained, courted with thirst
Are almost unstable and fall at the first
Silken flanks ripple with the satin-skinned
And dance to the sheepskin nose band

Eight out of tens
Dressed up to the nines
The much fancied fillies
The blinkered and the sublime
Teeter, totter, stroll and strut along the Melling Road

For this be the day of cut-and-slashed dresses
Kryptonite tights and evidence that less is
More sometimes, and more is less
Even the salad's dressed to impress
And giving it large in the noise and haste
With the willowy, the billowy, the good and bad taste
The tres chic, the faux pas, the fake, the designer
Erasing varicose veins with a Boots eyeliner

Glistening skin tones scrubbed up with glam balm
In pale-blue cashmere wrap-top calm
Decorated fingernails, full lips and eyes
Figure-hugging partners and those without ties
Gently squeezed into a malleable style
With the full nine yards and another half smile
As the wholly original and the freshly scented dream
Split their differences in variations on a seam

After a fashion we strike another pose
Happening then history with lace cup overflows
Cue the par for the course wearing fools you can trust
While the perennial well-heeled struggle with implant lust
Through the art of poise and improperganda
And make-overs done with an industrial sander

Snake venom facials
And collagen filler
Jimmy Choo shoes
Handbag and the killer
Dress with the Fake Bake
Flame-grilled aerosol can
That vital back-up in case
The crap hits the tan

Top tipsters in hipsters
The drowners not wavers
Necking hampers and champers
Vodka shots and Quavers
Fingers forming high fives
In the winner's enclosure
For falling off your slingbacks
And keeping your composure

There's horses for courses
The routine also-ran
The spirit-level headed
Mutton dressed as Spam
Silicon betting slips
With obstructed views
The half-leg wax
In ill-fitting shoes
Pre-cosmetic smiles
In an oasis of faces
Those who were there
But were not at the races

Manicures and pedicures
Worn medium rare
And a smorgasbord of headgear
And inflammable hair

Armani, Gucci, Tesco,
Gaultier excess
George at Asda, Westwood,
D & G , M & S
Prada, Versace
TK's and C&A
Aintree - Liverpool
Ladies' Day

Fat Happens

It's all over the telly
In all the magazines
You're nobody, nothing – you don't count
If you're not dead skinny it seems

And as we turn another page
In this rapidly fattening age -

The terminally obese
Are moved to tears
On forklift trucks
With grinding gears
While fast food lovers
Smeared in grease
Are mercilessly grilled
By the fried egg police

And late night clubbers
Model gastric band implants
Spending a fortune and a half
To get inside each other's pants

While those drip-fed images
Of the slender and the sleek throw up
More moaning Halloween skeletons
Than London Fashion Week
With their red carpet names
And size zero physiques
Telling us how to lose four stone
Inside a working week
Flaunting pale skin and bone
And a cold and deathly stare
All from living on diluted water
And the odd bowl of fresh air

As this world of unreality
Comes in and out of phase
The pursuit of thinness is galvanised
By Polly Filla clichés

It's very wrong, immoral
Unattainable and fake
Just let us stay healthy
And let us eat cake

Educating Ryvita

How Rita longed
For those faraway days
Of Chicken Madras
With stuffed naan bread
Chocolate-coated, full-fat
Peanut butter sandwiches
With lashings of
Middle-aged spread
And double cream cheese
With Pot Noodle potpourris
To keep her spirits
Soaring between meals
As she went her own way
Smoking forty snacks a day
Until she couldn't walk
And ended up on wheels

Amongst the latest fad diets
Made by saints for sinners
She'd had more salads
Than you've had hot dinners

But her devotion to cake
With ice cream and a flake
Was relentless with
A splash of unremitting
Her ever-widening frame
Put excessive stress and strain
On the NHS and most of its
Fixtures and fittings
So they put Rita on Ryvita
Now she's nine stone neater
And there's no more industrial
Scaffolding supporting her bed

She's back out spending her salary
On pleasuring herself with calories
As the lady says herself
You're a long time dead

The Real Slimfast Shady

'It's a matter of taste,' said the bull when he kissed the pig

This is the deal, it's real, I'm not fakin'
I couldn't do a day without fried egg and bacon
Polyunsaturates dressed in lard
I'm a black pudding, sausage and egg die-hard
A fried bread lover and a hot dog trapper
I once pulled a gun on a grease-proof rapper
But non-the-less, I'm non-the-wiser
Although I do exfoliate and use moisturiser

I need it now, I can't wait much longer
Full breakfast on a bap can only make me stronger
Make it or take it, you high-in-fat haters
You know where you can stick your baked potatoes
I'm not thick skinned, full of wind, sequinned and bloated
Even if my Parka is green and sugar coated
I know what I like and I like what I know
Get your bread in the tomato juice and go with the flow

Okay, we know life's better in dreams
There's no smoke without fire (except for smoke machines)
That flavour of the month only ever lasts a week
And the earth will never inherit Joe Meek
Tell me why 'abbreviate' is such a long word
Why honey gets a better press than lemon curd
But as a rule, keep your cool, if they call you fat
Don't let it get to you, you're bigger than that

I need you here and I need you right now
Two bread vans wrapped round a cow
You're the best at absorbing the night before
Why don't they kiss and fry-up like this anymore

This is real, it's the deal, and I'm not fakin'
I'm vacant and shakin' if I'm not makin' bacon
I need you here and I need you now
Two bread vans wrapped round a cow

I was in the planetarium with a vegetarian
In the butty queue behind an antiquarian
I laughed when he told me he could eat a horse
Especially if you rubbed it down with brown sauce
And unless I misheard or I'm very much mistaken
He was one of those veggie's that still eat bacon
Which serves to remind us, whichever way you re-heat it
Most of us want our cake and most of us eat it

I need you here and I need right now
Two bread vans wrapped round a cow
You're the best at absorbing the night before
Why don't they kiss and fry-up like this anymore
This is real, it's the deal, and I'm not fakin'
I'm vacant and shakin' if I'm not makin' bacon
I need you here and I need right now
Two bread vans wrapped round a cow

How To Belly Dance

Mix half a pint of gin
With a bottle of stout
Pull up your t-shirt
Roll the belly out
Consume the potion quickly
Get it down your neck
Unwrap any hip action
Concealed in your kecks

Grab a glass of whisky
Another vodka shot
Three pints of home brew
And quaff the quaffing lot
Then back shimmy, forward shimmy
Do the camel walk
Belly rolls, back bends
Roll the belly pork

Put the left leg in
Throw the right leg out
Do the whirling dervish
And another bottle of stout
Three Alabama slammers
A cherry brandy and a port
Then off with the sports socks
And the surgical support
And give it beans from the torso
Ignore the legs and feet
Undulate and gravitate
Across your own back seat

One Shakira
Two Shakira
Three Shakira
Four
Five Tequilas
Six Tequilas
Seven Tequilas
Floor

Luv etc.

A modern love song for modern song lovers

Please allow me to introduce yourself
You're the one I'd kill myself for probably twice
And even through those spells of lucidity
You're still the one I want, which is nice
It's you that I want to have problems with
You that I'd sell both kidneys for
I'd cut off an ear and eat my own feet
And set fire to my arse for an encore

When life seems nasty, short and a bitch
And happiness just an illusion
We can nail our colours and colour our nails
And bring the whole thing to a frothy conclusion
It's still feasible to be emotional
But it's impossible not to adore
The way that you always ignore me
With a Black and Decker cross-cut saw

Love, love, love, love
Love, love, love, love
Love, love, love, love
Luv
Love, love, love, love
Love, love, love, love
Love, love, love, love
Luv

I'm wrestling with what if's and maybe's
Blowing bubbles in the shallow end of life
On my hands and knees in a drawer full of spoons
When what I'm really looking for is a knife
But like bird shit on a window
And mucus on a sleeve
Me and you were made for each other
Have another sugar butty and believe

I Want You

There's butterflies in my stomach
And they're wearing barbed wire shirts
I've got toothache in both nostrils
Even my eyebrows hurt
I'm itching, breathless, can't keep still
I feel like a worn out shoe
I'm not too keen on the dysentery
And it's all down to you

I think my head's on back to front
My trousers feel too tight
I'm making socks from navel fluff
And I wet the bed at night
I don't know what I'm doing
But I know this much is true
I'm off my food and I'm off my head
And it's all down to you

You know I know
What happened to the lino
Underneath my feet
I saw and he saw
You on a see saw
Dancing indiscreet

I've lost all concentration
At times I struggle to speak
I've started playing bingo
Two or three times a week
I'm ten times tense and nervous
I've started sniffing glue
My imaginary friend's done a runner
And it's all down to you

And I want you
I need you
I want you
I need you
I want you
I need you
I want you
I really need you

To bugger off

Chalk and Cheese (Je Ne Regrette Rien)

Somewhere beneath the layers of joie de vivre
The Brie and Beaujolais, the syrup-tinted seventies shades
And all the fun of the laissez-faire
An obscured thought still curls its lip

With your alleged fewer wrinkles
Alleged firmer skin
And that haute couture gear
That you wrap yourself in
With your terminal coolness
And gastronomic delights
There's women wearing zoot suits
And blokes in kilts and tights
Like that John Paul Gaultier
And his razored bias cuts
One part genius
And three parts nuts
Jean Paul Belmondo
Yves Saint Laurent
J't'aime
Crap number one

Armpit fur, Les Miz
Red, white and blue
What's the 'must have' this week boys
Handbag or shoe?

Crusty bread, baguettes
Top reverse gears
Berets and onions
Narks that last for years

Joe le Taxi, va va voom,
Christian Dior bed socks
And that pasty-faced Marcel Marceux
Wallpapering a phone box

Comical toilets
Rancid stench
Dirty bastards
Excuse my French

Stripey shirts and Peugeot
Flouncing of the rules
Gauloise, film noir
Baggy kecks and boules

Renault, Citroen, fromage frais
Rousseau, Clousseau, Bastille Day
Chicken goujons, Le Coq Sportif
Holes for khazis, loads of grief
The odd revolution, Hectors' House
Garlicked-up, luke-warm scouse
Bardot, L'escargot, Depardieu's conk
Chapeaus and chateaux's, more onions and plonk

French Connection
Kecks and trousers
FCUK
Big boys' blouses

Cointreau, Metro,
Gateux, bolleau
Those who lead
And those who follow

French cricket, French chalk
French poodles, catwalk
French fries, French kisses
French horn, French Mrs.
French maids, French knickers
Non le Marathon! Oui le Snickers!
So you reckon you've got style to burn
And you say your love is king
But at the end of the day all I can say
Is piss off! It's a history thing

Sheena Is A Prawn Cracker

An exotic plum duff served with a gentleman's relish

Deep in the bosom of suburbia
Where the sweet and sour roam
Cat suits mix with Mao suits
And windows throw open the erogenous zone

A pair of old mingers with dark chocolate fingers
Are half dressed for cock tales at eight
Fruity and butch with that mandarin touch
Ming Dynasty on a plate

Enter Madam Butterfly
Tiger's eye, objectify
The soul of the beholder
Who nobody knows
In fine bone china
And pantyhose
She says yeah
Then no
Then maybe
Saying happy hour is nice
And warms up a spread
Of Yung Chow Fried Rice

A lone wolf with a well-thumbed menu in his hand
Ignites a nine dragon incense burner
A paper-hanging gent who hangs it out for Lent
Love you long time, happy returner

He calls out an order of salt and pepper squid
Laid out on a bed of mixed veg
And from the deepest recesses of his trouser
He pulls out a healthy wedge

Enter Madam Butterfly
Tiger's eye, objectify
The soul of the beholder
Who nobody knows
In fine bone china
And pantyhose
She says yeah
Then no
Then maybe
Saying happy hour is nice
And warms up a spread
Of Special Fried Rice

Playing snakes and ladders
From the bottom rung
Swapping sweet and sour
In a foreign tongue
Another Knight to Bishop
Taking out the prawns
Through herbacious borders
And manicured lawns
Gung Ho Kung Po
And Bo Diddley squat
Pasting the dragon
Embroidering the lot
John Wayne Chow Mein
Shoots 'em up again and again

While making a fist in the finger bowl
After deep fried banana in syrup
An aromatic jockey is thrown from his mount
His precious stones caught in a stirrup

Walking home the long way with an Elvis leg
And a trouserful of less than before
He'd kill for another sauced-up crispy duck
And whatever he could scrape up off the floor

Enter Madam Butterfly
Tiger's eye, objectify
The soul of the beholder
Who nobody knows
In fine bone china
And pantyhose
She says yeah
Then no
Then maybe
Saying happy hour is nice
And warms up a spread
Of beans shoots and rice

The Four Marys

1

Mary manned a burger stand
Beneath the Kop End lights
She flogged cold tea strained through the knee
Of her sisters' surgical tights

2

Mary had a little lamb
With roasties, peas and gravy
She'd picked up a thing for meat and two veg
From a bloke in the Merchant Navy

3

Mary, Mary, dumpy and hairy
How does your midriff grow
With pies, puds, pastries and spuds
And cream cakes all in a row

4

Mary had a little Lambretta
A souped-up sports 150
She used to do ninety up cobbled streets
'cos the vibe up her slacks was nifty

Crap Poem Number Two

Open all the windows
Bolt the khazi door
Drag down your undercrackers
Kick 'em on the floor
Drop the undercarriage
On the porcelain throne
Pour yourself a deep breath
And make your arse at home

Listen for the signals
Splutter with the drains
Steel yourself to detonate
The mustard gas pains
Gumshield in, seat-belt on
Bitter disappointment
A girlie number one

Then a bit of a flap, an audible snap
Static crackle baits your tackle
And plop goes the weasel
……. two voles, a stoat and a gassy ferret

But that glance in the bowl
At the guerrillas in the mist
Does nothing to disguise the fact
The stomach pains persist

Hand-brake turns and power slides
Bare-bummed roller coaster rides
Off the bog-seat and on the wagon
Crouching tiger, hidden dragon

And then, alone with the world's mysteries and obligations
And somewhat uncomfortably unannounced
A minor scuffle spills into the bowl
And even the doormen are bounced

Exploding popcorn
Eyes are dimmed
Rhythm and greens
Blowing in the wind
Sinking your teeth
Into imaginary leather
As your mainsail's torn
By the raging weather
And the remains of the day
Oh Jeez please rid me
Of this massive airlock
Staking out my kidney
There's raucous emissions
But no solid proof
Just a crack like a cat
On a hot tin roof

Sparring with your farmers
Then another big push
While shifting gear
With the toilet brush
Nostrils flaring
Spleen twisting
Face contorting
Eyeballs misting
Legs shaking
Knees knocking
Palms sweating
Sphincter rocking
Sinews straining
Everywhere

But you ride out the storm
Without gas and air

And then, without warning
A feeling of elation
You feel the nutty slack train
Pull into the station
So you gird your loins
Relax the trap-door muscle
While chewing on your lip
Ready for the tussle
A bubble and a squeak
And another number one
For additional protection
The shower cap goes on

With your tee shirt soaked
From the body heat
A twelve-gun salute
Rattles from your seat
Then one almighty push
Brings an end to the farce
As a flock of Hitchcock's starlings
Come flying out your arse

Physically drained
Like a fairground fighter
But soothed by the fact
That you're three stone lighter
It's a job well done
So you spark up a fag
While your arse-hole impersonates
The Japanese flag

Two rolls of Andrex later
Sprawled across the bed
The sound of the extractor fan
Spluttering overhead
With black-rimmed eyes
Looking gaunt and pale
Its kecks up, coat on
And back out on the ale

Peas And Love

Everybody's talkin' about
MDF
Diction
Haemorrhoids
Friction
Allergies
Curtains
Tesco
Burtons
Crap telly
Rock n' Roll
Healthy Heart
Self control
Pasta in plaster
And cars that go faster

Red cards, yellow cards
Alcopops a-go-go
Back page, front page
Rewind, slo-mo
Heart strings
G-strings
Pick n' mix selection
Russell Brand
And other resurrections

Body blows
Fructose
Nervous apprehension
Doubting
And spouting
Water retension
Flavours
And saviours
Boring repitition

Northern star
Caviar
Throwing up ambition

Should've beens
Might've beens
What ifs and maybe's
Could've beens
Would've beens
Men, boys and babies
Tactics and hat-tricks
And other frontiers
Comb-over jockeys
Dear oh dear
Get off the ale
And change your diet
Run your life
On peace and quiet
Eat your words
Have your say
Sell your cravings
On ebay

Kick the super lagers
The spirits and the stout
Because now staying in's
The new going out
Look after yourself
Get a grip of your dreams
Dilute your water
Eat more greens

And coleslaw
Bran flakes
Brown bread
Rice cakes
Consommé

Cauliflower
Bowel movement
Every hour
Grapefruit
Dried prunes
Short runs
Full moons
And ethereal
Cereal
That imperial
Material

And although nowhere near as desirable
As double chocolate creams
None of us should underestimate
The pulling power of beans
For healthy living
A rigid constitution
And an alternative to All Bran
Counter revolution

There's haricot beans
Red beans
Butter beans
Chilli beans

Should've beens
Could've beens
Might've beens
Would've beens

Never beens
Has beens
Runner beans
Broad beans

Kidney beans
String beans
Baked beans
Soya beans

French beans
Black beans
White beans
Green beans

But all we are saying
Is Give Peas A Chance

(Repeat until tape runs out)

Box

He lay under star-crossed covers
fingers numb, thoughts on fire

His eyes drew to a close
moistened and turned on themselves
polarising a depression
the cross to which he was brutally nailed

The silence burnt his flesh
distracting all distraction
but his head still screamed

and the terrors still terrified
as is the way when the violence of silence
has left you for dead

Head spinning, he called out
across the chill of the afternoon
desperate for a trigger
to help slip his skin

No visitors during visiting hours
no patience from the patients
words collapsed in slow motion
and a darkness kissed swollen eyes

Minutes became seconds
became days became hours
and thoughts became cages
locked for eternity

Then no words

nothing

only his possessions
in an envelope
in a box
by the
door

Café Society

Approaching elevenses from a southerly direction on
the A525 - and conscious of the Japanese proverb 'If
a man has no tea in him, he is incapable of understanding
truth and beauty' – I stop at the roadside to take tea.

Framed by long grass waving at foxgloves with dodgy knees,
a 1980's caravanette forces a smile, shabbily clad in several
shades of non-descript. In its shadow, a bad-on-its-feet plastic
patio set stretches its weather-beaten legs, its damp seats as

yet untroubled by trouser. Taking tea is not just physical but
mental - even emotional. Real tea. Tea with taste. Tea with
dignity. Inside the caravan of love, a pug-nosed tap dribbles
boiling water from the loins of a tarnished urn and fertilises an

assembly line of tea bags that queue patiently in polystyrene
cups. A full frontal fat fryer grunts in fluent monosyllabic, her
apron decorated with a rambler's map of the Yorkshire Dales,
laboriously hand crafted during numerous scuffles with snotty

eggs, brown sauce and the fat of the land. I smile and force a
polite, attention-seeking cough, but from behind a pencil
moustache, she fails to conceal the open wounds of a recent
charisma by-pass, as much pig is sacrificed to Arthur Brown,

the God of Hell Fire. Her top lip curls, unfurls and shouts up
another order while she makes a pig's ear of another bacon
roll. A white van man chances the patio set and hoovers up
a full English breakfast, his sleeves sweetened by the table

top sugar coating. A replica football shirt snorts a black pudding and
fried egg bin lid, the ruptured yoke trickling down his stubbled chin
and leaving him with little option but to clean his beard with a piece
of floury bap. Meanwhile, several muscular sausages hiss

their displeasure as the morning air is smoked out of its own back yard, forcing the pan to clear its throat, loosen its chest and snarl in readiness while the next bacon wave lies in state before another no-frills internment in this our daily bread.

But man cannot live on bacon alone. Given the fact that a good vet would probably have half of the frying pan back up on its feet, I skip the tea and leave with the feeling that there are things inside this van that Ray Mears wouldn't survive. Next day I bought a flask.

The Jimi Andrex Experience

'It's the first time I've been on a picnic,'
Shouted Joe into Mary's headphones
As he tried to freak out two mating squirrels
With a quick blast of *Kid Rock* ring tones

'Hey Joe, where are you going?' she said
'With that spam in your hand?'
'I've got a bit of stomach ache,' said Joe
'And the wind,' cried Mary, mid-handstand

After polishing off the sandwiches
And a selection of puff pastries
She suggested a game of kiss chase
In the shade of the silver birch trees
The cooler bag remained cooler than cool
As Mary became hotter and hotter
Joe was neither one thing or the other
So he picked up a pop gun and shot her

Slip of the Tongue

Adrenalin rushes of no fixed melody line
That flange and percolate in surreal time
And dance to the piper's nursery crime
Are warmed by the Gentlemen of Colour

With an underscore for the bigger bang
And a time-ravaged fistful of monochrome twang
A parcel of rogues, unwashed and unsung
Do the Methylated Spiritualists' slip of the tongue

2HB

She wanted to make a point. He had a point to
make. She sharpened a pencil with a penknife.
He wrote himself off in blue black ink. She
collected his thoughts from his trouser pocket.

He smoothed out the creases from another
half-smile. She thought he looked better on
Facebook. He thought she looked better from
half a mile. She looked at him. He looked at

her. She was beyond redemption. He was
beyond repair. She held the pencil like a dagger.
He held his nerve with both hands. She chose her
moment carefully. He gave in to her demands.

She picked up on his insecurity. He picked up on
her immaturity. She drew a matchstick man with a
token heart. He drew the line. She drew blood. He
drew breath. She drew a gun and left him for Ted

Disposable

To kill the silence, I speak. Quietly at first -
almost under my breath. But you take the words
from my mouth and throw them into the pedal bin
with the tea bags and walked-on eggshells. Your

heart - experienced and therefore composed in such
matters - avoids eye contact and blanks me. Mine -
cleverly concealed in my mouth - skips another beat
and begins to haemorrhage. I can feel razor wire

unravel in the pit of my stomach as you hurriedly fill
another bin bag with stuff. It's weird how significant
insignificant stuff can become given the appropriate
conditions. It all comes down to stuff in the end. I try

not to watch but risk one eye as the bags is pierced by
the stiletto heel of a wet-look shoe. Despite the
frustration, you skilfully double-bag, just like you'd
skilfully double-bagged so many times before while

packing the tinned stuff at Tesco. Unsure what to do,
I do nothing as the front door slams behind you,
blowing six years into the ether like a pall of cigarette
smoke from a discarded fag end. And I feel the passing

burn me. I look at the post-modern gravy stain on the
woodchip. The one that characterises the problemization
of pain and objective truth. The one that looks a bit like
a jelly fish playing the banjolele. The one created by a

flying sausage dinner during a chippy tea disagreement
earlier in the week. I'm overcome with a deep sense of
loss and my palms sweat, the inside of my head spins
through 360 and the questions - so many unanswered

questions. I try to rationalise but fail miserably. How could you do this to me? Where am I going to live? What's going to happen to the cat? How can I survive this brutal body blow with my dignity intact and still

keep a roof over my head? This is one of the problems in renting a room. If you get caught in the crossfire during other people's domestics, you become an involuntary, disposable bi-product of another broken home

.

Waiting For You

I've had home loans, exclusion zones
Ice cream cones, Toblerones
Contracts, peace pacts
Nik naks and ice packs

But in Bad-Dose-Of-The-Unrequiteds Land
I was only waiting for you

I've danced in the street
Kicked with both feet
Been stood up loads of times
Then given up my seat
Been ruthlessly betrayed
Fought a lost crusade
Worked all the overtime
And never been paid

I've played a ukelele
Round the back of my neck
Bobbled more crimplene
Than the cast of Star Trek
I've been candid, under-handed
Branded and stranded
Dabbled in humanity
Insanity and vanity

But in Bad-Dose-Of-The-Unrequiteds Land
I was only waiting for you

I've been a bit of a face
Had a warm embrace
Been high profile
Than sank without a trace
Been well off-hand
Had my driving banned

And developed a massive talent
To misunderstand

I've been a flying picket
And told them where to stick it
Been caught out loads of times
And clean bowled middle wicket
I've flowed and I've glowed
Had potential to explode
Had the route map in front of me
And took the wrong road

I've paid the going rate
been on a blind date
And attempted to mate
In a horrible state
I've been beguiled, re-styled
Read the works of Oscar Wilde
And after chicken vindaloo
I've had the bathroom re-tiled

I've been converter, deserter
Perverter, inserter
I've done the karaoke
With a kingsize frankfurter
I've been blessed, caressed
Stressed and possessed
And used a roll of gaffa tape
To wax my own chest

But in Bad-Dose-Of-The-Unrequiteds Land
I was only waiting for you

I've been locked in bogs
And chased by dogs
Danced on tables
In ill-fitting clogs

Played screaming solos
Sucked on polos
And stained my undercrackers
With some melted Rolos

I've used a portaloo
Had a small tattoo
I put Stardrops on my head
Because I thought it was shampoo
I've done the dodgy manoeuvre
Been a bit of a groover
And lost my pet hamster
Up the J. Edgar Hoover

I mumble that I'm humble
Give thumbs up to a fumble
And I'd walk a hundred miles
For my mum's apple crumble
I've had a muscle expander
Read all the propaganda
And had a game of naughty Scrabble
On my Auntie Kath's veranda

I've crept and I've slept
Been inept and then wept
Spent hours and hours wondering
Where the toilet rolls were kept
I've been down on my knees
Been out hugging trees
And my knowledge of biology
Would shock the birds and bees

But in Bad-Dose-Of-The-Unrequiteds Land
I was only waiting for you

I've been adored then ignored
Interested and bored
Showed a gap in my armour
And been put to the sword
I've hissed, kissed
Kissed and been pissed
I disappeared for six months
And wasn't even missed

I've ran on the pitch
Had a terrible itch
Kept things to myself
When I wanted to snitch
I've done the wine in France
Lost a cracking pair of pants
And been cured by a mystic
On the end of a lance

I've been blamed, framed
Drained and caned
I've faced a chair and a whip
But I've never been tamed
I've played, obeyed
Christ, I've even prayed
And loads of times on Saturday night
I've been mislaid

I've been a fierce campaigner
An active complainer
I've sent a sample to a doctor
In a molasses container
I've been existential
And influential
And when I put my mind to it
Inconsequential

But in Bad-Dose-Of-The-Unrequiteds Land
I was only waiting for you

I've played Russian roulette
Broken out in a sweat
Slept on a top bunk
Without a safety net
I've had a dribble, a nibble
A quibble and a scribble
And I would've been a Top Cat
But for Officer Dibble

I've had conviction and friction
Eviction and restriction
I've said yeah then no then maybe
Just for the contradiction
I've been shopped, flopped
And violently stopped
Then told I was rested
When I'd really been dropped
I've gone to ground
Been lost and found
Put my head in the spin-drier
For the surround sound
I've been cool, been a fool
Broken every rule
And been roasted in the cloisters
In a private school

I've had Armani suits
Three medieval lutes
And I've done the five day detox
With that stuff from Boots
I've been the soul of descretion
Stunk of Calvin Klein Obsession
Split the gusset of my kecks
Releasing pent-up aggression

But in Bad-Dose-Of-The-Unrequiteds Land
But I was only waiting for you

I've had the odd affliction
And suffered burns from the friction
Become Elvis in Vegas
Through a chocolate addiction
Been a man on a mission
A travelling musician
And flogged my dirty washing
At an art exhibition

I've been clocked, knocked
Mocked and shocked
Been blamed for the stench
When the sink was blocked
Been a coward, been empowered
Had it sweet and then it soured
And spent a fortnight up a tree once
With a crusty called Howard

I've been extreme, been supreme
Scored at Wembley in a dream
Been a guest at a wedding
With the urge to blaspheme
Been euphoric, alcoholic
Been considered shambolic
And sometimes when it mattered
I've dropped the odd bollock

I've been spent in a tent
Under the age of consent
I've lowered my defences
Then give it up for Lent
Been erotic, erratic
Occasionally ecstatic

And rolled over in the clover
With a Kodak Instamatic

But in Bad-Dose-Of-The-Unrequiteds Land
I was only waiting for you

I've been pushed, I've been shoved
Overlooked by Him above
Been savaged by disinterest
When it should've been love
I've smoked fags, worn rags
Lived out of bin bags
Stayed out beyond my curfew
In electronic tags

I've been down secret passages
Behind hidden doors
Been torn and bled inside my head
A rebel without applause
A dozen times the nearly man
With the whole world at his feet
Been there, done that, and got the scars
But lost the receipt

Head spinning, mind blown and senses bereft
You left me with nothing - and I've still got most of it left

So all things considered
And sadly this is true
I can screw things up myself dear
So bollocks to waiting for you

Honesty Policy

Say what you mean
And mean what you say
Even when the novelty wears thin
Once the toothpaste
Is out of the tube
It's a bastard to get it back in

Nauseam Ad

Male, 39. Considered ugly
Halitosis, glasses and overweight
Flatulent with erupting acne
Skin like a cheese grate
Seeks young woman, 18-24
Blonde, fit and slim
Financially solvent, with own car and house
To share his £10 Lottery win

Arthur

Arthur the carpenter was twenty two stone
And concerned about his health
So he boarded up his mouth
And shed half his body weight
Now he's a shadow of his former shelf

Harriet Loop

An alternative birdsong for those not remotely birdish

Once upon a couple of times
There was a girl and she was mine
If beauty's skin deep, this was real
She'd had a chemical peel

And so I took her by the hand
Kissed her on the hot dog stand
And underneath the sky at night
I felt her cellulite

With a crayfish and rocket sandwich in pocket
We re-played all night long
Drawn by her pelmet of strawberry velvet
I stayed for a crumpet with a butter trumpet
The like of which not seen since 'Last Tango In Paris'

She sipped her tea and dunked her scone
She said we two should become one
And slip inside the same warm glove
I said 'I don't do love'

She stamped her hands and clapped her feet
Had liposuction on Rodney Street
Puckered up in the cafe bogs
She'd been out kissing frogs

With her smoker's cacophony I couldn't get her off me
I dropped like a pumice stone
Romance is dead, this is what she said
It was strangled by men again and again
Who left women to clean up the mess

And so it came as no surprise
She disappeared before my eyes
She took the black and white TV
It didn't really bother me

I've got a retro radio now
And a slightly furrowed brow
I've grown to love an oven glove
Because I don't do love

Entrance Exam

We met in the hotel reception
She smiled twice without saying a word
Our attention was drawn by an artist called Sean
Who used most of his voice to be heard

'Due to the current economic climate
And I'm afraid none of us here are immune
The accommodation for the conference this year
Is two to a bed in each room ……. '

I didn't really hear too much after that
Due to the intake of breath from the floor
After balls were drawn from a velvet bag
A bit like the F.A. Cup draw

Number 32 – Exam Invigilator
Will share with …….
Number 7 – Performance Poet

What's that? Blimey – that'll be me
Sharing a bed with an exam invigilator
Is it my sobriety or does this Big Society
Need a six year old as a translator?

Seemingly oblivious to the ensuing hoo-ha
She smiled again without saying a word
Collected the key and pointed at me
All calm and undeterred

Up in room number 138
While she attended to her ablutions
I got under the covers in subdued light
And dismissed any chemical solutions

As we lay back to back
In reverse spoons
The darkness backlit
By two full moons
I thought about the weather
I thought about love
And I wondered what happened
To Michael Jackson's other glove

       Through amusement, bemusement
       Hypertension and pretension
       I bit my bottom lip until it bled
       I got up at least three times
       In the middle of the night
       Half an hour before I went to bed

But still she said absolutely nothing
And then she said even less
She was probably invigilating in her spare time
This examining body in a dress

But then, just after daybreak
She did what it says on the tin
Loudly and clearly she called out in the dark
'You may now turn over and begin .... '

The C Word

Sometimes it's hard to say what you mean
Even harder to mean what you say
Without accidently using the 'c' word
Which at best is more than risqué
When used in everyday parlance
It's a word that can shock and offend
For some, the 'c' word, *committment*
Means the beginning of the end

Relationships are tricky at the best of times
We're all well aware of that
But what is love if not an opportunity
To have a fifty per cent share in a cat
Something to throw money at willingly
With an upper hand over clenched fist
So we can share in someone else's perfection
If, indeed, perfection it is
When you're having and holding
On to loves' young dream
Changing duvets and unfolding
Another Dulux colour scheme
It's maddening one day
And majestic the next
But you know that she loves you
She said so in a text
But while you're washing the dishes
And taking out the bins
One day you'll wonder whatever happened
To the sound of violins

There's the moaning, groaning and criticism
Petty jealousy, fist fights and mood swings
The age old dilemma of openly breaking wind
That accompanies not only the exchange of rings

But cohabitation, living together, sharing a living space
With the fear of the joint bank account sketch
Weekends spent lapping the garden centre
Praying for your patience to stretch

The butcher, the baker
The mover, the shaker
The crusty and dog on a string
The scholar, the geezer
The dressed up to please 'er
The joker, the Queen and the King
The doctor, the healthy,
The skint and the wealthy
And probably the Man in the Moon
All walks of life and the world and his wife
It seems nobody is immune
From making the wrong decision
And then leaving the scene in a rush
But whether committed or sectioned
You get tarred with the same toilet brush

Sometimes it's hard to say what you mean
Even harder to mean what you say
Without accidently using the 'c' word
Which at best is more than risqué
When used in everyday parlance
It's a word that can shock and offend
So only use sparingly after taking advice
In the meantime, smile and pretend

Life's Like That

Whatever it may throw at us
From the peaks to the lowest trough
Life is like a pubic hair on a toilet seat
Eventually you get pissed off

Whole Lotta Nothing

A half-arsed rant to the tune of your savings

I'll have to love you and leave you
Because I don't believe you
About you and that white van man
It doesn't take all night
To fix a pilot light
And unblock an avocado toilet pan

You stayed up talking?
He's hardly Stephen Hawking
Come on, you're having a laugh
I've heard it all now
You're just a horrible cow
I'm going home to drown in the bath

Have I cut off my nose to spite my face
I've got an angry rash all over the place
And I just can't seem to get myself into gear
But then again, this is life
Half-full of emptiness and full of strife
Bollocks - I won't even bother to shed a tear

I'll play Wreckless Eric all day long
Now I'm the singer and I'm the song
I'll give it large in the land of plenty
I'm surfin' on the crest of a slump
And I haven't half got the hump
I've just peeled a banana and it was empty

Yeah, I was down but now I'm up
It's only the norm in a teacup
Everyone knows you can't keep a good man down
So it's head up, chest out
Chin up, school's out
Let's clear the table and sink the pink and brown

That's just the way it goes
It keeps you up and on your toes
It's all part of life's warp and weft

But live for today
No matter what they say
And at the end, have a look at what's left

A Whole Lotta Nothing

Frankie Goes To Halewood

It was the day after tomorrow, and the start of the
beginning was already seven minutes late. Frankie
rolled up his sleeves and pointed at the clock with his
foot. 'It's going backwards,' he muttered, as a minute

leapt from the mantelpiece and disappeared down the
back of the coal bucket. With eyebrows singed, he sighed
a long sigh alongside himself, and sized up the possibility
of seismic activity. Smouldering slightly, he dampened down

a small fire in his trousers and peeled off the remnants of a
flame resistant shirt. Unfortunately, the receipt had perished
during the big bang so a refund was unlikely. His nostrils
buckled as the lingering smell of his hard-boiled lunch box

collided with an angry stench emanating from the pedal bin.
He knew from experience that things could get a lot worse
before getting worse still. Not withstanding, he sat down
three times in his artificial hipsters, and each time it sounded

like a firework going out. He wasn't getting any younger
and every day brought with it an impressive array of trouser
experiences. He glanced at his watch and another two minutes
blazed along the dado rail and disappeared behind the fridge.

After a quick flick through the TV Quick, his eye was drawn
to a half-moon of congealed marmalade curled around a button
on his trousers. The preserve was like granite – harder than dried
Weetabix – and he knew the situation would demand a surgeon's

precision with a pickled onion stabber if the button was to be
freed of its ginger beard. He set to work. Despite fists of ham,
fingers of butter and a minor problem with gas and air, the
operation was a complete success. After a final spit and polish,

Frankie felt an overriding sense of achievement riding over him. He carefully brushed the marmalade dust into his handkerchief and smiled contentedly, celebrating the optimism that inevitably overwhelms when enjoying such

an enviable standard of personal hygiene – particularly after a small explosion. He picked up his dentures and composed himself on the Stylophone, secure in the knowledge that attempting to light a Café Creme on a camping stove that

uses a volatile liquid fuel in a pressurized burner whilst wearing stilettos and a paper party hat (breathe) probably wasn't a great idea. He pulled a loose flap of skin from his chin and sighed, his cockles warmed by the thought of his redundancy money.

Cloudburst

Now you've packed your bags
And moved in with the plumber
Having ripped out the boiler
The kitchen and the bathroom suite
There's things I need to know
Things that just don't make sense
And it's costing me at lot more
Than beauty sleep

Why didn't Tarzan have ever a beard
When he was living rough in the trees?
Isn't bad luck bad luck enough
Without turning up in threes?

How do you know when it's time
To tune up bagpipes?
Who decided that navel fluff
Should be blue?
Why is there a light in the fridge
But not the freezer?
And why do motorway hard shoulders
Only have one shoe?

You left me a troubled soul
When you downed tools for the plumber
But there's something you should think about - and this I know
One swallow doesn't make a summer

Apache Appendix

There was something grumbling under Daniel's jumper
It was growling and snarling next to his dinner
And it soon became plain as it dished out the pain
There would only be room for one winner

All under his vest was soon under arrest
And his stomach blew up like a footie
His insides groaned while his bum coughed and moaned
And his belly refused a chip butty

So he fixed a stare on his navel
And tried to inflate his morale
While grumblin' Apache Appendix
Lit fires up Jim Jams Chorale

It was all going off big time
Abominable abdominal grief
So he lay in his bed while inside his head
His tongue snuggled up to his teeth

But help was at hand from a medicine man
And by the light of a slippery moon
The feel good professor removed the aggressor
With a spanner, some jam and a spoon

Now there's nothing grumbling under Daniel's jumper
And there's plenty of room for dinner
So bring on the fries, the pizzas and pies
'cos now he's three shoe sizes thinner

Strawberry Fool

They hang around in punnets
All red with bit of green bling
They're very rarely on their own
The gang mentality's their thing
They're heart-shaped, plump and fragrant
But things have gone seriously awry
Because even in extra strength varifocals
We don't see eye to eye

I look at them
They look at me
And we give each other daggers
With a lifetime guarantee
And I can feel all my allergies
Coming on stream
They're testing my resolve
And testing positive for cream

When I say yeah
They say no
When I say stop
They'll shout go
I'll say up
They'll say down
I'll say city
They'll say town
If I call it in
They'll call it out
If I say flood
They'll say drought
If I say hot
They'll say cold
I'll say rocked
They'll say rolled

I'll say swim
They'll say drown
I want to laugh
They want to frown
I'll say skin
They'll say bones
I'll say Beatles
They'll say Stones
I'll say north
They'll say south
I say gob
They say mouth

So now there's nothing left to say
It's there for all to see
Every which way you look at it
Strawberries don't agree with me

Daze

it wasn't a great day
got up - got undressed

made a cup of tea
de-caffed and de-stressed

closed the door in my pyjamas
opened the mail with a spoon

lost all interest behind the settee
found yesterday afternoon

picked up the paper
put down a revolution

stopped the clock radio
started my ablutions

stood by my principles
sat on scattered cushions

shouted out the letter box
whispered through concussion

blocked a fiend on Facebook
unblocked the outside bog

ran the bath
walked the dog

pushed the boat out
pulled another muscle

polished off the biscuits
cracked a crossword puzzle

questioned the phone bill
answered the phone

gave a definite maybe
received a dialling tone

filled half the kettle
emptied most of my head

looked in the fridge three or four times
went back to bed

The Girl With The Lazy Eye

A torch song without any batteries in the torch

Forget black holes, pension schemes
Politics and footie
Office drones, corporate slaves
Mr. Benn and Sooty
This cartoon has a heart
And it's me who finds the rent
But it's never pumped up
It just loiters with intent
And it's all your fault
It's all on your head
I blame you and shame on you
For leaving me for dead
I wanna prick your conscience
I wanna make you think
You can lead a horse to water
But you can't make him sink

One day, one sunny some day
You'll come and find me
Cut the ties that bind me
And one day - it's not that far away
You'll come and show me
The eye to eye you owe me
The rules are there aren't any
And there never were
I was dying for us to work
And you were dying your hair
You were wired and active
And I was weird and passive
Giving it excess all areas
With the down the pub massive
I was looking to twist
You were looking to shout

And now even the tide
Wouldn't take you out
I can see we were entwined
But never joined or whole
And your soul and my soul
As one became our soul

One day, one sunny some day
You'll come and find me
Cut the ties that bind me
And one day, and it's not that far away
You'll come and show me
The eye to eye you owe me

Dark Side Of The Spoon

The chairs are moved
And tables turned
Tumbling dice roll from the gods
Along feint lines of heavily-typed bullet points
The bigger they are the harder they fall

Swollen eyes burn
Red-rimmed, half-closed
As reality - Hitchcock-esque, steals through the shot
Unsecure in the knowledge
That they mustn't keep meeting like this

Heaven's Door half-opens
And double-fazed windows close
Another shot of entente cordiale is diluted
By cautionary tales that melt in the mouth
And linger on the lips like a devil's kiss

And the flickering flame
Still throws back its tangled head
And drinks the moonlight in the midnight air
Medicinally inseminated by the brown sugar
On the dark side of the spoon

Adios Libido

It wasn't the phone you didn't pick up
Or the words you didn't say
It wasn't the hand you didn't hold
Or the promises that went astray
What really hurt was your lack of belief
That together we could leap any hurdle
Especially with your Ann Summers loyalty card
And my discreet man-girdle

So it's no more banana Angel Delight
To greet you from work every day
I won't be there to fix the crack of dawn
Or repair the break of day
That's me – I'm done, I'm off, had enough
And I want to make this crystal clear
Recently you've made me feel as welcome
As a hang-glider with diarrhoea

Sometimes I forget how sensitive I am
And because I don't know all the words to life
I make them up, improvise, hum the chorus
And live on the edge of a knife
While you're as sharp as a transvestite's stiletto
And while it pains me it's come to this
You can take the boy out of Liverpool
But hey - you can't take the piss

Talent

I was a real talent - that's what she said
Refined, intelligent and smart
She loved my sense of humour
And my passion for bacon and art
Never forgot my birthday
Not once in all those years
And she never ever used bad language
Without sending rubber bungs for my ears
She got locked up for attempted murder
Her solicitor informed me by letter
She tried to kill Keith Chegwin with a frozen chicken
Thank Christ I never met her

Chained Melody

By the dishwasher, in the bowels of the kitchen
Near the heart of the state-of-the art
A face wears a trace of adrenaline
Another cycle invites a kick-start
As she carefully feeds the front-loader
Gently closes the door
And tries to remember what happened
To the girl she was before

With cheekbones like geometry
Shrink-wrapped in cellophane
And eyes like Gene Wilder's caught
In the lights of a runaway train
She fondly remembers her first love
The raised heartbeats, the romance
Then opens the machine and throws in
Another pair of soiled underpants

But then, in a moment
As she peels the rubber gloves
Her life flashes before her
On fast spin with lost loves
As she chisels off the Weetabix
From the breakfast bowl
And wonders how it all went begging
Down the plug hole
All those years, those hopes
Those dreams and ambitions
And those home front propositions
In unforgiving conditions
Twenty winters and more
Of near solitary confinement
Thank God she's raised the necessary
For the gender reassignment

Pauline's Hat

Pauline's hat
Is where it's at
It's made from footprints
And a dogtooth cat

It makes you look splendiferously
Omnipotent with a dash of sublime
And a least a foot taller with less of a limp
I wish Pauline's hat was mine

Ascension Day

Between the cornflakes and the aspirin
The dog rough and the smooth
Dental floss and parking fines
Each day, tongue-in-groove
We inhaled each other's laughter
Even coughed in a similar key
I was thrown together for you
And you were made for me

I grew to like our mutual friends
The ones you'd know since school
Your lunchtime boob job looked the biz
In short, I thought we were cool
And then one day, there you were gone
I found a note in the biscuit jar
The postman saw you drive off with a bloke with a beard
And a fish symbol on his car

It seemed I was losing everything
You, the plot, my head
And because you said suffering is the only path to truth
I listened to a whole CD by Simply Red
But still I'm none the wiser
As to why you left that day
And I can only thank your God for Connie from the Chippy
And Lucy, Mandy, Jackie, Jenny, Jill, Louise and Fay

Loose Change

You can change your clothes, change your tune
Change your mind in a changing room
Change your car, your socks, your phone
Change the fuse when your lights have blown
With a change of heart, change no to yes
Change direction and change address
Change the duvet, change the world
Change your allegiance when the flag's unfurled
Change your route and change your plans
Change your name with a change of hands
Change your identity, change your kecks
Change your appearance, change your sex
Change your tactics, change your style
Change a frown into a smile

Winds of change, climate change
Life-changing dreams
Change is inevitable
Except from vending machines

More Syrup On The Sorrow Pancakes

Dislike
Animosity
Aversion and revulsion
Antagonism
Odium
Disfavour with repulsion

Detestation
Repugnance
Contempt and disaffection

She thoughtfully wrote this little note
To help me with the rejection

All I Want Is Everything

All I want is everything
It's not too much to ask
But if it is, your savings'll do
With some Hobnobs and a flask

Lazy

I'm epic in my laziness
I thought I was borderline M.E.
Turns out I just couldn't be arsed
Medical science eh? Bugger me

Apologies To Rupert

If I should die
Think only this of me:

That's that bastard dead then

Genetic Engineering

Colin's infidelities
Were not his fault it seems
He was driven to distraction
By something in his jeans

Net Result

The family tie-breaks
Across an umbilical net-cord
Symbiotic players play out the final light
Visibly weakened by each debilitating volley

A failing offspring falls beyond reach
Limbs seize and fail, lips tremble
And eyes like still waters
Moisten and run deep

And the forehand passing shot
Returned in the past tense
Having written
Moves on

Death By A Thousand Cuts

To be or not to be
That is the question
With you or without you
And the mental indigestion
That interrupts my sleep at night
And punctuates each day
With question after question
While the concrete and the clay
Beneath my seat begins to crumble
Waiting for the axe to fall
If there's a time for divine intervention
This would be the best time of all

Looking for a jump start
While the lights are fused on red
All sense of balance senseless
From the first cut to the head
You've never been the singer
Never listened to the song
And every day's discoloured
By so many shades of wrong

So we react to one another
Like a slug reacts to salt
There's livelihoods on death row
And none of it their fault
That dubious honour lies elsewhere
Pressing the flesh in bars
It's fingers on lips and hands on head
Ignore the mental scars

You cut me adrift
Cut me to the bone
Cut me to the core
Cut the ring tone
With cuts to the eye
And cuts to the lip
Cuts that tore the heart
From the intravenous drip
Prime cuts and choice cuts
Roughly cut and paste
Cuts to the wrists
And cuts to the face

Cuts to the air supply
Cuts to the veins
Cut from the same cloth
Time and time again
Cuts to the house
Cuts to the home
Cuts so deep
They hit the bone
Cuts to the jugular
Cuts to the chest
Cut-throat razor cuts
Cuts on request

Cut to the present
And the economic map
You can't cut the mustard
If you don't you cut the crap

To be or not to be
That is the question
With you or without you
And the mental indigestion
That interrupts my sleep at night
And punctuates each day

Oppressing and suppressing
The things we need to say
Demanding demonstration
Heart and pride and guts
Or we roll over – die - concede defeat
Death by a thousand cuts

Politics

We've had big guns, setting sons
Propaganda re-runs
Sound bites, bang to rights
Televised fist fights
Pivotal rolls, opinion polls
Cheese and smarm on crusty rolls

Extensive expenses and flimsy defences
Embroidering reality with assorted pretences
To protest and survive, connive and contrive
With a desire to be wanted, dead or alive

In through the side door, out through the back door
Seals on deals made real on the dance floor
Majorities, priorities and the trading of places
And musical chairs to re-arrange faces

    Staying, going
    Reaping, sewing
    Gloves on, gloves off
    Kicking in, kicking off
    Lock-ins and shut-outs
    Shut-ins and lock-outs
    Departures, arrivals
    Closures, revivals
    Love-ins and love-outs
    Mood swings and roundabouts

We've seen contempt redressed as love
Unlikely bedfellows hand in glove
Affecting lives, souls, confidence and complexion
But still no treatment on the NHS for a dysfunctional election

Valentine

Every single second of every single minute
Of every single hour of every single day
Of every week, of every month, of every year
At least three times, quite often four
I never think of you

The Girl I'll Never Forget

How could I ever forget
What's her name?
You know, the girl from
Was it number 63?

She had long red hair
Or was it short and brown?
Always drinking coffee
Or was it tea?

She used to love playing tennis
Or badminton - or was it chess?
Always wore jeans and a leather jacket
Or was it beads and a cheesecloth dress?

She sat next to me once on the bus
Or was it opposite on the train?
Sent me a postcard from somewhere in France
Or was it that letter bomb from Spain?

Anyway, you know the one I'm talking about
Her with the house in Mustique
Or is it Middlesbrough? Or Manchester? Doesn't really matter
It's our decree absolute next week

Paradigm Valentine

Books are read
Trumpets are blew
I love you madly
And so do you

Kook

Dear Nigella
Let's talk about you
The way you gently smoulder
In your pulchritudinous stew
With your lustrous, raven tresses
And dark, chocolatey eyes
That more than fabulous frontage
And your slavering passion for pies
Oh la stupenda of the blender
Amongst the bland also-rans
How I yearn to lift the lids
On your non-stick pans

There's something about you
That juices a desire
Arouses the trousers
And flame grills a fire
All thrusting, wild
Exciting and beautiful
Lusty and mild
Biting and dutiful
It's your whole demeanour
Your style and your taste
And your resemblance to a photo-finish
In a zeppelin race

Your conker-shiny spare ribs
With pineapple and molasses
Poaches my appetite
And steams up my glasses
My legs turn to Chardonnay-flavoured fromage frais
At the thought of your flapjacks on a baking tray

You've made me epicurious
With your culinary burlesque
Your diet-killing cheesecakes
And sherried chicken breasts
Your sensuous, full milk chocolate mousetrap
Finger-licking spread
If you can't get my pastry to rise
I'm probably dead

The Most Wonderful Time Of The Year

Get dressed ye sherried gentleman
It's light and Christmas Day
The morning after the night before
There's things to undo and say
A bird in need of stuffing
A sack of spuds to peel
Veg to be strained and neatly rearranged
And a trouser stain to conceal

But time and tide waits for no man
Or Norman, his half brother
And while the mother of all hangovers
Was hanging all over his mother
The exasperated current Mrs. Norman
All orange face, pink neck and perky
Ignored the temptation to kill a mocking bird
To stuff a bantamweight turkey

All decked out with rubber gloves
And a bin bag of sage and onion stuffing
She inhales another glass of Diamond White
To calm her nerves after a night of rebuffing
And gathers herself as best she can
From all four corners of the room
Wishing that she could be that lucky cow
That ran away with the spoon

Meanwhile …….

On a pasting table in the kitchen
A bird with the build of Sly Stallone
Blows its parson's nose on a tea towel
Pulling on its own wishbone
The cat pulls a mussel from its wallet

And the clock flicks two fingers at the wall
As the relatives arrive by the skin full
And kick off the fighting and crying in the hall

As another senseless lass looked out
Full of yeast and heathen
Alcopopped to buggery
And lippy all uneven

At the same time ....

Old Ebeneezer, a diamond geezer
Takes a tumble in the snow and is imprinted
There is much delight as he's a miserable sod
And a miser too, he's minted
Jolly Mr Jump and a rusty bike pump
Was adding petrol and lime to the punch
To fuel the adventures of his ill-fitting dentures
The perfect aperitif before lunch

Jammin' with Jacob Marley and the Wailers
After a game of quoits with Ms. Frizzell
Uncle Roderick eats his odour eaters
So when Christmas kissing starts his breath won't smell

Dancing Mr Ryan sends a gravy boat flying
And a pint of giblet stock burns through his truss
He skids across the floor astride the cutlery draw
Sounding uncannily like Don Partridge getting off a bus

'Fear not,' he said, 'for Mighty Fred
Had seized his Simple Minds LP....... '
But he was talking broken biscuits through a mangled cullender
And most definitely concussed - probably

Ginger ninja Michael is the life and soul
And believing that God loves a trier
He stands on his head and plays the sousaphone
With his ding dong merrily on fire

A burst pipe later ....

Dicky and Vicky Forfar from number 44
Purveyors of hot gossip and fine rumours
Vicky being squiffy gives Dicky a wedgie
Severely bruising his satsumas
People would pay to see Aunt Emily play
After forty odd sprouts and counting
She bends over backwards in front of the fire
And blows smoke rings through her sherbet fountain

Gauging, scratching, biting, bitching
And a serious assault with a frozen chicken
It all kicks off big time when the office party rumours
Reach ruthless Aunty Ruth in the kitchen

Unforgiveness, jealousy , anger and resentment
Are microwaved with remnant of mince pie
While the bloke from next door gets all the kids to promise
To denounce Satan, the Moonies and McFly

There's another attempted murder in the bathroom
An unsavoury incident with a saveloy on the stairs
Another trouser accident is induced by home brew
And there's a stabbing during musical chairs

An electrical fire sparks up the Christmas tree
A fist fight breaks out over the punch
A plumber's blow torch fires up an old flame
And there's still an hour to go before lunch

But time still waits for no man
Or Norman, his half brother
Legs akimbo in the baby's bath
While his formidable significant other
Head butts Uncle Charlie in the little boys' room
Emotional on eggnog, gin and beer
Thank Christ it only comes around once every twelve months
This most wonderful time of the year

Resolution No.9a

This year my resolution is to get more sleep
And lie down and be counted as another black sheep

I'll sand blast and pipe clean most of my thoughts
And stop effing and blinding at the match reports

I'll learn a foreign language and kiss a stranger
And vigorously exfoliate in the face of danger

I'll look for happiness and not court sorrow
And I'll procrastinate more - starting tomorrow

I'll adopt a hippopotamus at Chester Zoo
Get a back, sack and crack job and a small tattoo

I'll knit a balaclava from navel fluff
Watch more TV - I've been missing some good stuff

I'll give up blue cheese and embrace a mild Cheddar
Go to McDonalds and order a McSpreader

I'll banish negativity and any self doubts
Walk along a beach with a large bag of sprouts

I'll gain loads of weight, at least half a stone
And refrain from upgrading to the latest mobile phone

I'll spend more on moisturiser, less on clothes
And I'll be more discreet when I'm picking my nose

I'll think more about others and less about me
And finally find the best place to position the settee

When faced with provocation I'll turn the other cheek
And I'll give up eavesdropping for three days every week

I'll stop telling fibs and tell the truth. Amen.
And I'll never, ever make New Year's resolutions again

January

She looked at her reflection
In the back of a spoon
A sort of cross between Madonna
And the Man in the Moon

While he wrestled with the lid
On the Marmite jar
And wondered if the police
Would ever find his car

And the HD ready TV
Refuses to transmit
Only the cat's got it sussed
Doesn't give a shit

Another minute does a runner
And is never seen again
But every minute has its moments
And this was one of them

Adjusting his pyjamas
He takes up the slack
Catches her eye
Throws it back
Holds her attention
Squeezes it tight
Relaxes his midriff
And presents this invite

'Let's stuff the turkey butties
And the gluten free ales
Let's go and blow my redundancy
In the January Sales
Come queue with me
And be my love

At Selfridge's
Where we can shove
In amongst the cracks in the flags
Throw the blanket down and the cooler bags
There's some cracking bargains
To be had at this time of year
Furniture, luggage, luxury towels
And that designer gear
You could knit yourself a wind sock
To while away the hours
Make a bin-bag wigwam
To ward off the showers
Take a barrow load of butties
Ham and egg and cress
Your duck down sleeping bag
Pose for the press
We could snuggle up and gaze
At the winter stars and dream
About how the Victorians
Made things out of steam ……. '

In less than a moment
She was ready at the door
But second thoughts had kicked in
And now he wasn't sure

'There's just one thing that worries me
When nature takes its course
What do you do, where do you go
When you need to water the horse?
There's not a lot a bloke can do
When your waterworks get naughty
And there'll be loads queuing in the queue
The dusty side of forty
We need to think this through
You could come a cropper
If your bladder swells up

Like a space-hopper
It's a terrible predicament
One we all dread
When you're dying for a pee
It really messes with your head
Becomes almost spiritual
Not something to abuse
And I was always brought up
To mind my P's and Q's
Nah, on reflection
It's not a good idea
What with the all the weather
At this time of year
Let's replace the PP9's
In the back of the transistor
We'll open that bottle of Creme de Menthe
And have a game of Twister ....'

She looked at her reflection
In the back of a spoon
A sort of cross between Madonna
And the Man in the Moon

While he wrestles with the lid
On the Marmite jar
And wondered if the police
Would ever find his car

The HD ready TV
Still refuses to transmit
But the cat's got it sussed
Doesn't give a shit

January

Child

When voices raised have died
Unpeacefully in their sleep
And big boys' toys thrown
Unnecessarily from the pram
Look into your child's eyes
See yourself
And smile

To Do List

There's lots of things I need to do
Before I shuffle off this mortal coil
Swim with dolphins off the Mersey Bar
Bring Nigella Lawson to the boil

Abseil down the rusty side of Blackpool Tower
Fly to Runcorn in a microlight plane
Drive coast to coast on Route 66
Circumnavigate the earth by train

Drink a bottle of mescal in Mexico
Get my body into optimum shape
Sleep in my underpants under the stars
Let Catwoman peel me a grape

Ride a camel to the Pyramids of Giza
Dive from the highest diving board
Leave a risque poem in a library book
Pull a communication cord

Have my portrait painted by Rolf Harris
Play draughts in a game of chess
Learn to say 'yes' when I really mean 'no'
And 'yes' when I really mean 'yes'

Fillet a fish with a Swiss Army knife
Make a brand new hole in a belt
Smash a plate glass window with a sledge hammer
And allow what's left of my heart to melt

Make a perfect one egg omelette
Do my laundry in the Ganges
Cross a glacier on a unicycle
Play Twister with Siouxie from the Banshees

Fire an elastic band at a traffic warden
Give everything I own to a mate
Climb an active volcano in flip flops
Establish a utopian state

Watch News 24 for 25 hours
Ride a lightening storm at sea
Fit three weeks work into three days
Buy another Yamaha FS1E

Overeat in Italy for three and a half weeks
Sell everything I don't need twice
Break wind loudly in a confined space
Admit to being afraid of mice

Visit each of the seven continents
Stay up for at least 48 hours
Bring something home from the local tip
Steal a forecourt's worth of flowers

Eat a whole bucket of steamed mussels in Bruges
Write a fan letter to Mohammed Ali
Get arrested again for a minor offence
Buy a Champion Jack Dupree CD

Lose a week's wages on the slot machines
Think myself taller and thinner
Enhance my reputation as a ne'er-do-well
Drink myself unconscious over dinner

There's lots of things I really should do
Before I'm measured for the wooden overcoat
But the truth of the matter is I can't be arsed
Quote - unquote

Smile

The same in any language
Powerful, contagious and free
A smile is worth a thousand words
And comes with a full warranty

It's the shortest distance between us
When all is said and done
If you see someone without a smile
Stop and give them one

This Supporting Life

What is this life
if full of care
we have no time
to stand and swear
as the season comes
and the season goes
and expectation
overflows
are unblocked
not by the hand of God
but by blokes in boiler suits
from Dynarod
amidst the ooohs, the aaahs
the ifs, the buts
the games, the names
that drove us nuts
the should've been
could've been, nearly men
the winners, the sinners
and those times when
that promise of nirvana
that something in the air
was substituted early on
replaced by despair

Nine months in season
delivered full term
with lessons in love
that we never seem to learn
through unflinching devotion
home and away
it's hard to keep a lid on it
you've got to have your say
and hand out the accolades
dish out the dirt

we've all been there, done it
kissed the badge, got the shirt
and we know why we do it
there's millions of reasons
even the immortal bard
had a man for all seasons
there's the incidents, the upsets
the casualties, the drama
the highs, the lows, the comatose
the good and bad karma
and those times when we drew
when we knew we should've won
when we were under the moon
instead of over the sun
and we still believe we'll learn from this
and come back even stronger
maybe add to the squad
if we attract a bit of wonga
so come next August
when it all kicks off again
we can move on from the worry beads
to the Little Book of Zen

Lady Ga Ga Meets Right Said Fred

Raise your glass to the goal celebration
That debatable, inflatable show of elation
Forget about the handshake and the pat on the back
Now you can get your kecks off just for the crack

Front crawl, back flip, shirt above the head
Lady Ga Ga meets Right Said Fred

You've got the critical analytic
The dancing paralytic
The mover, the improver
The impossible manouvre
The stronger, the conga
The short and the longer
The audition, the magician
And the position in the mission

Front crawl, back flip, shirt above the head
Lady Ga Ga meets Right Said Fred

Then there's the immune, the lampoon
The laying it on with a spoon
The ambitious, the auspicious
And the boring repetitious
The circus-style showstopper
Verging on the improper
The rumble, the stumble
And the accidental fumble

The adorer, the ignorer
The richer, the poorer
The ironic, the harmonic
The chronic sardonic
The glorious, laborious
The send them victorious

The warmer, the informer
And the half-arsed lukewarmer

Front crawl, back flip, shirt above the head
Lady Ga Ga meets Right Said Fred

There's the floater, the voter
The lower league bloater
The emotional, the notional
The arrogant self-promotional
The persued, the subdued
The shrewd and the tattooed
The spouting, the shouting
And the kiss-me-quick pouting

The fiddle and the doddle
The 'Forgive Me Father' Hoddle
The uncertain final curtain
While going for a burton
The prone to brag, the cabaret gag
And the X Factor audition with the corner flag

Front crawl, back flip, shirt above the head
Lady Ga Ga meets Right Said Fred

        There's the keeper, the sweeper
        The mascot Grim Reaper
        The huddle for a cuddle
        Swan Lake in a puddle
        With a bit of a dive
        And a jukebox jive
        Then hands in the air
        For another high five
        To kiss the crest, bare the chest
        And the illegible slogan on your big girls' vest

Front crawl, back flip, shirt above the head
Lady Ga Ga meets Right Said Fred

And what about the struggle, the snuggle
The dancing partner juggle
The squeezer, the sneezer
And the 'come and chase me' geezer
The almost regal
The just about legal
The felled, the gelled
The jet-propelled
The yeller, the teller
The three crates of Stella
The resplendent, the transcendent
The toilet attendant
The drifter, the shifter
The serial shirt-lifter
The shredder, the threader
And the bend-over spreader

But let's have some perspective
So what - you've scored a goal
You haven't housed the homeless
Or taken millions off the dole
You haven't saved the planet
Or spread peace from east to west
I'm bored to death now - just shake hands
And give all this crap a rest

Front crawl, back flip, shirt above the head
Lady Ga Ga meets Right Said Fred

Great Expectations

The Football Association Challenge Cup Final

Upon a Calvin Klein Obsession flavoured pillow
Uneasy lies the head that craves the crown
Because today's the day it's gonna kick off big time
Today's the day the gauntlet hits the ground

The alarm clock kicks in
And you're caught out of position
Tackled from behind
By Stevie Wonder's 'Superstition'
You dribble in your lucky pants
Around the bedroom floor
The ones you've worn for every game
Since 1974
Jockey with the cornflakes
And several cups of tea
A shower, a shave, a too-tight shirt
And another number three
Grab the lucky rabbit's foot
And sprigs of lucky heather
And a Tesco bag to put on your head
In case of inclement weather

Then it's out with the boys
And inflatable toys on the road to glory
Anecdotes, footnotes
And the elaborate Jackanory
Crack another six-pack
As your colours are flown
Then a coalition's u-turn
'Cos you've left the tickets at home

But straight from the re-start
You're back into the groove
With re-mixed chants from yesteryear
Complete with dodgy moves
While ever-swelling bladders
Require a master tactician
As once again you're caught offside
In a promising position

To the edge of the thrilling fields
Unable to relax
With tension and bravado
Like a Working Men's club act
Swallow a few more lotions
To galvanise the nerves
And a bag of greasy fish and chips
To aid the body swerves
Squeeze through the turnstiles
And settle into your seat
For this live one-off performance
Starring victory and defeat

Dressed up, fired up
Made up and messed up
And all inside the first sixty seconds
Temperamental, ironic
Judgemental and sardonic
As the middle finger of fortune unfurls to beckon

To celebrate or lament
To dance like a Dad at a wedding
To flash your Maltesers
Or kick your own head in
To cry yourself a river
To wear a jesters hat
To hug the bloke behind you
Or become a loudmouthed twat

To be or not to be
That's always been the question
To believe or not to believe
Beyond the indigestion

Through thick and thin and thinner
We forgive and we forget
When dreams we buy into are shattered
By some blokes we've never met
It's just the way it's always been
Once bitten by the bug
Because this really is a love thing
And that love is the drug

The Football League Cup

V-necked cotton jerseys
Rosettes and beef tea
Pitches topped with treacle
And Brylcreemed referees
Players with proper names
Like Arthur, Frank and Ray
Giving it legs in black and white
Home and away

Swinging London haircuts
Heading the lace
The original people's final
Opened arms to embrace
Big boys and smaller boys
In different coloured threads
Fighting for the right
To throw you up above their heads

But the heads were getting bigger
The orders getting taller
The shirts getting tighter
And the shorts getting smaller
But still they called for Brasso
And a soft cotton cloth
So that when they got you home
They could polish you off

And though you're all embracing
And make no class distinction
Some European bounty hunters
Called for your extinction
That they'd all had a piece of you
On the way to greater things
Is a v-sign of the times
And the disrespect it brings

As you were born
The brainchild
Of an aggregate
Two-legged affair

They forced a conical hat
Upon your head
But you still managed to find
The jaunty angle

So shall I compare thee to the FA Cup?
Thou art lovely and even tempered
Perhaps a bit more knobbly and squat
But so long as men can breathe or eyes can see
Let us rejoice for all time in your fine extra handle

And although many
Have caressed you
Held you aloft
Ran their rough hands
Through your ribbons
Aye, 'tis true -
Few now remember
Your birth name
As you seem to be
Down at the Registry Office
Every other year
Pledging thy troth all over the place
And taking another's name

Milk, Littlewoods
And Rumbelows darling
Coca Cola, Worthington
And a dalliance with Carling

But thy eternal summer will never fade
As unlike those darling studs of May
You always peak early, in February now
First in, first served - fair play

Life's A Pitch

All the world's a pitch
And all the men and women merely players:
They have their exits and their entrances
And each in their time will suffer
From the slings and arrows of outrageous misfortune -
The staggering decisions, the well dodgy penalty
The 'obvious to all in the ground but the ref' handball
The variety of anxiety
The athletic and the pathetic
The prolific, the terrific
The at times scientific
Offsides, onsides
Added time, out of time
From life at the top to avoiding the drop
Ah, this infectious disease; this high-wire trapeze
This Premier League; this England

Game On

Monday's game was full of suspense
Tuesday's game a needless expense
Wednesday's game was full of woe
Thursday's game - didn't bother to go
Friday's game showed some potential
Saturday's game was existential
Sunday's game turned out to be a winner
A bottle, a floozie and a roast beef dinner

Another Littlewoods Carling Coca Cola Milk Cup Uncle Joe's Mint Balls European Second Leg Semi-Final Second Replay Tetchy Terse Ticket Knock-Back

Having queued on a full bladder
Without complaint, butties, bickies or a tartan flask
For at least five and a half hours plus stoppage time
I finally make it to your little portakabin window

I snuggle up to the plug-hole in the perspex
Uncurl a well-rehearsed, if slightly inane, introductory smile
Speak slowly and clearly through the little perforations
And without looking up you tell me I'm not on

       I chew a semi-splutter
       And I swallow a cough
       And weigh up the possibilties
       Of maybe kicking off
       But I resist the urge to nut the glass
       And with much emphasis on diction
       I calmly fondle my worry beads
       And say with some conviction

I've got the four special vouchers
Three yards of industrial strength gusset elastic
Sixteen Curley Wurley wrappers from the seventies
Five ticket stubs against teams raised on Marmite soldiers
Two jars of 'No Frills' extra large pickled gherkins
Four chunky hand-knitted toilet roll covers
And a fully working mechanised otter

There's a sharp intake of breath involved
As you shake your head, like a plumber sizing up
A tricky no-job-too-small, while preparing the way
For the two-footed-two-fingered-jaw-dropping estimate

How can I be discarded
Dismissed, red-carded
Ineligible and persona non grata?
I go to every single game
Through the wind and the rain
I should be lauded and applauded as a martyr

You look up from your indifference
Sigh one of those sighs that plague
The terminally inconvenienced
Lean forward and, through what looks like
A wind-induced half-smile, say -

This is charades and fan cards
And postal applications
Adult and child re-unions
'Category A' inflations
Executive leg room up-grades
For the battery hen stand
And the official supporter's club credit card
With the highest APR in the land
This is for those paying through the nose
For a seat with an obstructed view
So you're wasting your time here, fella
You're in the wrong bleedin' queue

I'm rooted to the spot
Drained, tired and dull
Overcome with a confusion
That adds a calmness to the lull
And as I try to disguise an Elvis leg
I'm bursting for a pee
You lob your voice over my head
In the general direction of not me

'NEXT!' you shout
Convincingly

A Study In Scarlet in Royal Blue Biro

*A rose-tinted backwards glance at the 1986 Liverpool Everton Cup
Final*

Before Alice bands, scrunchies, goggles and glasses
Tights and gloves and corporate passes
Two colours alike in dignity
Left a lipstick mark on the memory

Almost twenty five years ago today
Though Sergeant Pepper wasn't called upon to play
A study in scarlet in a royal blue biro
Was written in words of our own

And though we never walked hand in hand
It's not good form on a one-afternoon stand
We were caught without rift standing side by side
In awe of what fades so soon

They were bathed in limelight and wrapped in the hour
Cometh the communion, cometh the power
A hometown and its landscape unfurled upon green
To fuel a collective fire

We bought and sold banter in the same currency
Were swept off our feet by the choreography
Safe in the arms of each other's trepidation
Individual, abstruse and compelling

With blue touch papers lighting two-touch sparks
We'd played this game ourselves before on bygone parks
Out of the blue, into the red and beyond that purple patch
Both flaunting a familiar side

Bleached into the memory, lest we forget
That day we spent together, that day we last met
And hearts broke and spirits soared
For this is no ordinary love

And now this emotive beauty, more dignified with age
Still tugs the heart and turns the head as we turn the page
We're older and wiser, bolder and wider
But the flavour is enhanced by time

Before Alice bands, scrunchies, goggles and glasses
Tights and gloves and corporate passes
Two colours alike in dignity
Left a love bite on the memory

Derby Day

I've got this little problem
I don't want to say too much
But I've got another dose of the old nemesis
It's a sore point and it's sore to the touch

And I know when it's gonna consume me
The day, date, time of day
And despite antibiotic dramatics it's always
When Liverpool and Everton play

It distorts the emotional well-being
And your sanity well, that does a runner
Mild apprehension starts snarling with tension
And your bladder's on the blower for a plumber

It two-footed tackles your eyesight
And throws up a neat turn of phrase
You scream at the ball with gestures an' all
And start coughing up threadbare clichés

It's outrageous and really contagious
And there's only one recognised cure
Ignore the strong liquor, argue and bicker
And pretend you're content with a draw

Red

The hereditary route to the miracle of Istanbul

There's no defining moment or singular event.
No suddenly seeing the light. No spiritual calling
from deep within. This is in the blood.

It courses through the veins, is passed without
warning from father to son and becomes ever more
precious as each year passes. This is a birthright.

Overseas adventures and expanding dominions lie
floodlit in the memory, all vibrantly coloured and
skilfully woven into the fabric of place and culture,

drenched in history and preserved for all time. And
nobody did it better. In everyday lives, the power
and the glory years still move within, where faith

tackles reason two-footed and takes away the breath.
Somewhere, North West of Eden, what was once
rooted in the here and now became painfully trapped

in the amber of history. But the merest hint of only
one of a glut of abiding memories is all it takes to
rekindle those passionate, stomach-churning,

enthralling nights spent together. In your heart of hearts
you always believe in belief - you re-ignite the red touch
paper and stand close. Cue the alchemist - minutely

detailed and chipped off the old block – summoned to
contemplate past glories, destined to confound the Euro
sceptics. All journeys begin with a tentative first step -

then a second - then a third. The guiding hand re-writes
the bristling scripts, each one a highly-seasoned drama
of crackling tension. Grown men struggle to hold back

the tears and hangovers have never been enjoyed so
much. Yes! Love is in the air! And the timing could
hardly be sweeter. Amidst mosaics and frescoes, the

magic carpet ride continues to astonish, as beguiling
and unfathomable as ever, only now with an extra
resonance and a new beauty. This is what it's all about.

Through emotional smithereens
And splintered scenes
The appliance of defiance
Serves to galvanise dreams
These blazing apostles
Aren't shaken but stirred
And all with an accent
Exceedingly rare

This is what we're all about. Intense, mad, fervent
passion! We should never have gone our separate
ways, never have lost touch. Oh Big Ears! God is

a Scouser! And he's shown us that tear-in-the-eye
fairytale endings really do exist! Enough of kissing
strangers – let's gorge ourselves on Turkish Delight!

With that Liver Bird upon your chest
When push comes to shove
I don't care too much for money
Money can't buy you love

And a million miles from the miracle of Istanbul, at the
business end of Walton Breck Road, after six minutes that
shook the world, even the traffic lights are stuck on Red

This England

They mess you up
The England team
They may not mean to but they do
They play with your emotions
And colour your language
Red, white, but mostly blue ....

World Cup Blues

Fermented to perfection
Across four long years
The nation's collective psyche
Juggles hopes alongside fears
Itching daily scratch cards
Understanding what it means
To slide tackle bacon
Sausage, egg and beans
For that no-nonsense
All day full English vibe
Under the moon in June
When we're encouraged to subscribe
To the biggest shooting party
Where old flames are re-ignited
And thanks to the plasma on the chimney breast
Everyone's invited

Roast beef, cup of tea
Stonehenge, the mushy pea
Shelley, Nelson, Wordsworth, Milton
Churchill, Fish and Chips, Ray Winstone and Stilton

Front page news swaps
Shirts with the back pages
Plot nutmegs sub-plot
As football fever rages
National anticipation
Unfurls its bingo wings
And just for the hell of it
Hope eternal springs
As the countdown warms up
For the World Cup and his wife
And those who've never seen
A decent kick-off in their life

Brilliant and bracing
Articulate manoeuvres
Tactically aware sweeper systems
Employing Dyson hoovers
Salt and pepper pots
Are moved around tables
With tales of metatarsals
From Aesop's Fables
Pavement debates deliberate
On the starting eleven
Players play the lottery
With spent pennies from Heaven

News and views on injury blues
And trouble between the sticks
And endless references
To nineteen sixty six

Ant and Dec, garden gnomes
Green and pleasant, Sherlock Holmes
Vivienne Westwood, red meat
Wallace, Gromit and Heartbeat

It doesn't matter who you are
Or whatever it is you do
You can't help being drawn in
By the red, white and blue
When England half-expects
You consign, you commit
So you can stand up with pride and say
'I saw it - we were shit'

All England Expects

Apply liberally to affected areas – particularly football and tennis – at least once a year

The flags unfurl and England expects
And the question that tumbles from everyone's lips
Is one we've tasted so many times before

You can feel it unravel on unmade corners of half-smiles
That frisson of expectancy, that desire and hunger
To strive for things we'll probably never own

With the salad dressings come the mixed summer blessings
Pouring light and warmth upon the memory of paradise lost
And those half-eaten, unanswered questions fall from open mouths

So much need and want wrapped in fist-clenching bravado
We're happy to pay through the nose in emotional currency
So we may breathe more and sigh less

With hopeful and well-rehearsed false harmonics
And parting shots that give an illusion of possibility
Perhaps we help and hinder in equal measure

Through rose-tinted, we watch as potential courts talent
And we feel their pain as they struggle to exchange vows
To form a lasting union : to exist as one

The Joy Of Six

Six Nations with oval-shaped balls

Stand off all the clocks
Hand off the phone
Line out all those memories
The ones we all co-own
Of who and what
Where, why and when
And if at first you don't succeed
Try and try again

We watch from the wings as the drama unfolds
Throwing a brilliant light across dark winter months
Fuelled by an extreme strain of belief
While understanding at any moment
The rug can be pulled by those unseen hands
That lie knuckle-deep in gauntlets thrown down

Edgy, beautiful and anointed in the slurry
And wrapped in the heavens' embroidered cloth
Tight heads loosen a running stream of consciousness
Of wide men and wide boys
The outstanding standing out on fields of fire
Where possession is nine-tenths of the law

Hearts of like-passions are worn on soiled sleeves
Trading delicate blends of blood and spirit
In that common market place
Deliberate in speed and with majestic instancy
For those who hint at great deeds must surely be roused
As that which does not kill breeds strength

Tackles crash into the abdomen like a leaded fist
Their heavy application causing both wings to unfurl
While immersed in the comfort of chaos

Line outs line up like reptilian dancers on a hot plate
As friends, Romans and countrymen
Lend us their cauliflower ears

Degrees of flamboyance grasp raw power
And surges through the ranks without sentiment or apology
A collective response to outclass and outgun
While the back row re-cast prop idol
The definitive reality show

A crimson close-up cut to the face
Cuts to the chase
With a dummy, a side-step
A killer burst of pace
Handbrake turns and power slides
Highs converting lows
Sustained attack, shuffling the pack
Under psychological blows

Engulfed in competition
Committed and driven
Each half no quarter asked
And no quarter given
Exhilarating innovators
Prophet, seer and sage
Game on, game off, peace on, peace off
Let the nations rage!

So stand off all the clocks
Hand off the phone
Line out all those memories
The ones we all co-own
Of who and what
Where, why and when
And if at first you don't succeed
Try and try again

Cue The Balls

Keep one foot on the floor at all times

Oh my love's like a red, red, red
That's newly stung from the baulk
With miscued dreams of paradise lost
My cue devoid of chalk
As fair art thou, I shall return
To embrace those hallowed halls
And with one foot firmly on the floor
I'll sink those coloured balls

But there's things to attend to behind the scenes
To pot a sporting chance and realise your dreams
You want stamina, strength, a perfect technique
A piston-like action and a ruthless streak
To tighten your defences, sharpen your attack
And get out of the red and into the black
Kissing mellow yellows, stinging the blues
Pocketing brownie points
In the pink and in the news
While living a healthy lifestyle
With strict dietary regimes
A sallow complexion? Not enough greens

If you want to be taken seriously
You've got to look the part
So get yourself a waistcoat
And look dead smart
With a pair of those kecks
With the tram lines up the side
A slim-fit shirt
Get your neck bow-tied
And the shiny shoes
Sensible and steady
Even if you look

Like your mum got you ready
Then a leg over the table
To show what you can do
Sipping tap water
And polishing your cue

And in the raked seating
As they calculate the score
A stifled cough is frowned upon
You're not allowed to snore
Because silence is golden
It serves to enable
The Harry Potter potters
Work their magic on the table
Working out the angles
With the extra dimension
It all adds flavour
To the drama and the tension

Stomach-churning, table turning
In-off steely nerves
Off the cushion, off the rails
Stuns and spins and swerves
Ability, fragility
Of mice and men
And those little scribbles on the screen
With the magic pen
To show the safety shots and parting shots
The cue for position
Trick shots and long pots
Almost exhibition
Thunderclaps and lightening strikes
The maximum break
The plant and the kiss
And the costly mistake

One day we'll go then, you and I
To the great green table in the sky
Where heavenly nights in smoke-filled halls
Couple those with cues to those with balls

Athlete

All truths wait in all things
And fragility remains in the balance
As hubris and nemesis make sport of human ambition
Rehearsed without sorrow and lost with a trace
Like an Achilles heel in a world without feet
Where success is counted sweetest by those who'll never succeed

Cleanliness is next to godliness
And a spirit that can soar loses track of all else
While flesh and bone arrows through the humidity
Unfurling a succession of brief, amazing moments
Where breath and accolade are taken in equal pleasure
And hidden emotions set free

Exquisitely brooding and driven by a rhythm
Thrilling beyond words bursts from the blocks of miracle and
wonder
The unexpected resurrected and those who teeter on the cusp
Jostle with bounty hunters and the dashing and daring
While new talent snaps at the heels of those outnumbered
But so rarely outgunned

Self-imposed pressure tumbles from roughly-hewn shoulders
Sipping through the heart of once-still waters that long to run deep
Into harmonious coexistence in fast lane or on hard shoulder
Brilliantly lit by past glories flickering through the filter of time
The body of the god and the folly of the mortal
Clock-watching as one

Chewable tension races through the minds of the well-assembled
Where fear of the unknown stretches and stands its ground
Demanding the shout when whispers fall short
And forcing the hand of the record-incinerating fire-starters
To relay intrigue and incident spilt from the lap of the gods

While crafting works of lasting value
Bound by the burning sting of cascading sweat
Through eyelids closing, the alchemy unfolds its wings
And after one fleeting, final glance – has flown

Olympic Standard

Anticipation flexes muscle
In the warm summer air
As the most civilised meeting
Of nations prepare
Although the heart of the motherland
Remains resolute
The Olympian dream
Courts disrepute

A long-running, drug-fuelled
Multi-layered story
Follows those who give chase
After the ultimate glory
It's not always the grafters
Who'll run until they drop
But those who've got access
To the best chemist's shop

From nowhere to somewhere
In the blink of an eye
From out of the running
To machines that can fly
Random dope testing
Calls talent into question
By those with an interest
In an athletes' ingestion

Along with the shock waves
There's quiet satisfaction
Among the cleansing agents
In the front line action
Who really do take the piss
During well-aimed tests
To sort out what really lies
Beneath those numbered vests

Perhaps we need to look beyond
The wealth and the fame
And the record-breaking record breakers
Now and again
For the reasons that so many
Are willing to yield
Simply to compete
On a level playing field

They've got to get a grip
But where do you draw the line?
I've heard a cup of green tea
Could constitute a crime
And all those pumped-up additives
Can cause all kinds of grief
To those caught off their blocks
Who beggar belief

But in this pick n' mix counter-culture
It's far from clear
Which everyday pick-me-ups
Can shatter a career

There could be places in races
For big smiley faces
Brought on by Senatogen abuse
The Germoloid wide-eyed
Would crack open a broad stride
As the multivits worked themselves loose

And then like a bat out of nowhere
Some skinny little bloke from the back
Could do 0-60 in a second and a half
Speeding on Fiery Jack

And a line of talcum powder
Prescribed for athlete's foot
Could seriously put your nose out of joint
If someone else made the cut

And those heavy-legged-never-was-also-rans
With no hope in hell of ever showing
Fuelled by a good dose of laxatives
Could get the locomotion flowing

To be the fastest on earth
Is the ultimate aim
If you want to reach the zenith
The top of the game
Itching for the starting gun
Imagine the thrill
To break the land speed record
On Vagisil

But those anointed with greatness
And those undoubtedly clean
Those finely-tuned, fully committed
Magnificent flying machines
Can take some consolation
From the Greek word catharsis
And put these cheating bastards
On the bones of their arses

Cheats never prosper
They can run but never hide
And when judgement day arrives
And these two worlds collide
Only those on adrenalin
Will push beyond their limit
On nothing more sinister
Than pure Corinthian spirit

Flights of Fancy

World Championship Darts and shirts to savour

As true as the arrow
That flies by day
The spoils the victor will claim
But watch the unknown, they're never thrown
Take heart, take hold and take aim

Bring me a board of burning gold
And those arrows of desire
A brightly-coloured polyester shirt to unfold
And a fulsome belly full of fire
That I may walk amongst you
While the stereotypes distil
And ponder why some overlook
Your talent and your skill

There are no flights of fancy
No corporate stuff, it's just a game
When all said and done
No lovely-super-smashing-great
Look at what you could've won
Just a retro-in-your-face honesty
With a thrusting lust to entertain
And as people are playing it everywhere
This must be the people's game

No delusions of grandeur
To forget or forgive
A local game for locals
Wherever you live

With real drinks, proper food
And no sign of a prawn sandwich
With partisan support from passionate crowds
And the chance to extend your language

How many other sports
Can embrace us all
Where you don't need a jock strap
And you don't need a ball?

I've got the stance, the glance
A killer pair of pants
And I've picked up the vibes a treat
I can throw in a spanner
Clamour for the glamour
And dance to Jocky Wilson's 'Reet Petite'

I've got the character, the showmanship
The razzmatazz, the charm
And a life-size Barbie Doll
Tattooed on my arm
And if everyone's honest, hand on heart
We've all had a scuffle with a tungsten dart
Be it 301 or round the headboard
We've been there, had a fling
And some of us have scored

One day I'll straddle the oche
And eyeball the treble 1
Stand with legs akimbo
And call out 'Game On ……. '

The Boat Race

While daylight washes down on silver water
Angular blades, classically symmetrical
Make their incisions in perfect phrase
Each one choreographed with pathological enthusiasm

Steel nerves are exposed to the elements
All powerful and curiously affecting
Tearing through the waters' skin
Towards the glorious, billowing wave of victory

Aintree

From the comfort of the Armchair
Miles from the Canal Turn
Maybe the absence of Google Earth
Was once a cause for concern
But as the Liver Birds unfurl their wings
And take the strain of expectation
Informed and articulate insight
And cultural observation
Now displaces that old tired criticism
Once written by the yard
Because now the going's good to firm
The naive are suddenly jarred

It's not just the accent
That's exceedingly rare
If you're into cathedrals
We've got a cracking pair
And with the cultural capitalists
To explode the myth and rumour
Sorting out the purist
And the casual consumer
The geography has never changed
For the wise man or the fool
Aintree is and always was
Aintree : Liverpool

So with the crocus, the daffodil
And the rambler's right to roam
A nation's anticipation blossoms here
With the gambler's right to moan
As all walks of life commune
And gird their girdled loins
Their imaginations captured
Along with their coins

There's a feeling in the water
And something in the air
Harnessing a desire to win
With all the fun of the swear
The binoculars of the world look on
And yet, for what it's worth
Form books fly from windows
The technique shall inherit the earth

And whether experienced campaigner
Or an absolute beginner
Everyone's got an outside chance
Of picking out the winner
That's the way it is and was
That's the going goes
It's why we get that urge
To stick a fistful on the nose
Or throw even money each way
On a swinger with the girl next door
On a horse with teeth like a bloke she met
On holiday in Singapore

As well the unbridled excitement
There's the money you can make
Although you wouldn't be the first or last
To fall and die at the stake
When there's sandbags in saddlebags
With go-faster stripes
And unexhausted-looking horses
With twin exhaust pipes

It could be the jockey's colours
Or a name that takes the eye
That 1000-1 outsider
That's convinced you it can fly
Or well-washed silks and satins
In colours that look like they'll run

Or that photogenic dark horse
That looks like a young Red Rum
The well-backed favourite outsider
That's been on and off the rails
The thoroughbred, courageous hot-tip
That runs like a donkey and fails
The moody stable-filler
That's held in high regard
Picked by method 301
A dart in the race-card

But winning isn't everything
It's the taking part that counts
But whoever said that's brown drinking vouchers
Hadn't disappeared in large amounts

So if your disappointment's startled
And ruination's chomping at the bit
Tell yourself that all's not lost
Just most of it

Cut to the Chase

The Grand National Steeplechase

Spring comes to consciousness
And sets the pulses racing
Across the good to firm of these thrilling fields
Where plot twists extend beyond the mortal realm
And moistened palms crease betting slips
Between fingers crossed

Outlined against a blue April sky, splendour falls
Times present and times past are simultaneously inhaled
Memories and impressions collide
And distort those with loftier pretensions
When course becomes kingdom
And saddle becomes throne

Shifting tensions and ravishing moments
Are gift-wrapped in a brief encounter
And money where your mouth was slips off the nose
Through sweeping highs and crumbling lows

Absolute trust is met with absolute betrayal
For those on the champers and those on the ale
Immersed in an emotion that has to run its course
Through the steely heart and courage of the horse

The curious, the quirky
The beautifully named
The natural born thrillers
The well-campaigned
The against all odds
The lightly-raced
The silk and satin dancers
The ever well-placed
The hard to fancy

The run-of-the-mill
The born to be wild
The born to thrill

The rhythm and speed kings
The mythical flying horse
The progressive chasers
The par for the course
The emerging dark horse
The top class stayer
The overweight sensation
The dead cert player
The rookie and the bookie
Talking monkeys and ponies
The top ride form guide
Believable and phoney

The commotion of emotion
The first to show
The electric sprinters
The ready, steady, go
The sheepskin noseband
The blinkered view
The four-footed tackles
The too-good-to-be-true
The ripple of muscle
The pound of flesh
The old, the young
The tired, the fresh

Owners, trainers, runners and riders
Dead certs, favourites and fancied outsiders

Binoculars, monoculars, telescopes and glasses
Trilby's, camel coats and corporate passes
Pursed lips, dodgy tips, the full SP
And tactile tic-tac tactics with no guarantee

With that tension and intensity
From explosion to chase
You've got to have a flutter
On this unique race
It stirs the blood
Stiffens the sinew
And could tease out a latent
Lucky bastard within you

Walk This Way

Olympic Racewalking

With a level head and a relaxed jaw
Ankles flexed to keep one foot on the floor
They cultivate the heel plant while flexing the pelvis
And twist like a chorus line in those 60's films with Elvis

The heel of the hands brush the hip bone
And raise the beats-per-minute on that long walk home
Satisfying, precise, percussive and robust
The primary flexors, the also-walks, the sussed
Wearing beautiful contortions that cut beyond the chase
Their inner-soles shuffling at a blistering pace
In smooth and synchronised great strengths of feet
Real hip action in the groove down on the street

The dashing and the daring, whipped on by adrenaline
While camaraderie walks hand-in-hand with the will to win
Tinted sunglasses raised in celebration and, as is the fashion
The slickest of footage illustrates the beauty of pride of passion

With a level head and a relaxed jaw
Ankles flexed to keep one foot on the floor
They cultivate the heel plant while flexing the pelvis
And twist like a chorus line in those 60's films with Elvis

Xpelair

Wimbledon - The grunting phenomenon

Handsomely shod feet baseline dance
And during the pre-service ball-bouncing
You can almost hear a pin drop a point

After a couple of slight knee-bends (apparently it's in the rules)
A favourite ball, the one picked out after squeezing all the others
Is skilfully tossed skywards

As it drops in mad-dog heat
Highly-strung graphite, wound up and fully loaded
Rears its head to show its explosive side

But as impact's moment arrives
And the wrist snap comet
Hurtles through blurred vision
Something other-worldly warms the ears

It sounds like someone blowing up a lilo
On a moped at full throttle
While expelling gas and air
Through the neck of a water bottle
And it's not just a one-off blow out
Because each and every shot
Is cheek by jowl with guttural growl
Like a bulldog chewing a wasp

And it's not a gender-based phenomenon
'cos both the women and the blokes
Are capable of lobbing in
These grunt-assisted strokes

There's the groaners, moaners
And imbalanced hormoners
High-pitched squealers
And mystical self-healers
The open to question
With grumbling indigestion
Racketeering schemers
Coughing absolute screamers

So what exactly is going on
With the groans and moans and snorts?
Is it ill-fitting lycra all-in-ones
Or too-tight y-front shorts?

In times of sheer frustration
We all offload the odd scream
Like when you can't get the top off
The reduced fat salad cream
But there's nothing to suggest
You get the edge on an opponent
From being a fully paid up
Freestyle grunting exponent

Is it a source of power
Or a timing thing
Does it fine-tune your focus
Clear the throat, help you sing
Can it make your game soar
Like a bird on the wing

Nah ….. I don't think so

It's just a deep and meaningful expulsion of air
A statement of intent coughed up into the air
And while individuality is definitely worth a shout
Whatever it is that's pissing you off, come on - spit it out!

The High Chair

Wimbledon – The Umpires

Perched in a lofty position
In a high chair surrounded by faces
(not unlike those for small people in bibs
in the more child-friendly eating places)
There's nostrils that recognise chalk dust
And those miss-nothing-all-seeing eyes
Ears that can smell an expletive
When lobal warming applies
'cos precision with vision in every decision
Is a guarantee, their ultimate aim
They guide and decide and studiously preside
Through strawberry-tinted spectacles and rain

Disputes, altercations, tantrums and cafuffles
There's no job too big or too small
And with a heightened sense of   timing
They never take their eye off the ball

You wouldn't sit in the high chair
Exposed and with nowhere to hide
With only a green blazer to conceal the frustration
That surely must fester inside
When you call the court to order
And the jury's on your case
You wouldn't sit in the high chair
You wouldn't take their place

So when it's all going off big time
And it's easier to get up and go
With only the clouds above us
And the barley water below
It's the same as it was in the beginning
Is now and shall be evermore
Whatever they say is gospel, okay
Deal with it – they know the score

Keep On The Grass

Wimbledon - Praying for the antidote to disappointment

On the edge of the solstice
As summer approaches its height
The nations' collective pulse-rate smoulders
And our hopes and dreams re-unite
On a wave of nationalistic fervour
Unrelenting in its desire
To deliver us from expectation
And although God loves a trier
We share each others' longing
For someone we can class
As a genuine contender
To keep on the grass

SW13

Wimbledon – The Spectators

Side by side, their faces blurred
They cut through the highly-strung tension
Singles and doubles wrapped in warm apprehension
The court in session, the outcome deferred

Back-packs and panamas
Sharing passion that burns
The absolute beginners
The many happy returns
Those who remember
The wooden Maxply
Whitening for your Green Flash
And Cyclops' other eye

The relaxed, the flirtatious
The warm and the cool
The fashioned and the casual
The advantage point rule
Court cases, handbags
Tea and champagne
The unexpected déjà vu
Pleasure and pain

Side by side, their faces blurred
Devotion undimmed, mindset unaltered
Game after game after game
Where love means nothing at all

From Bad To Verse

Wimbledon – Tactics for making the Final

Sponsorship logos and All England whites
Wrap a reinforced gusset and surgical tights
With my serve and volley a definite maybe
I look like you could beat me with a ukulele

Despite foot in mouth, trench foot and no teeth
Some serious weaponry lies underneath
Beautifully handcrafted from the finest maturity
To lull you into a false sense of security

I use swerve on nouns on the forehand
And batter adjectives over the net
I put top-spin and slice on my verbs (which is nice)
And take consonants to a fifth set

I'll serve a sentence down the line
And return with a vengeance throughout
But when white-hot passes
Smash Hawkeye's glasses
And the rhyme judge calls it out
Is it wrong to write an opinion
Jam a paragraph into reverse
To fire from the lip
And completely let rip
As things go from bad to verse

I'm often erratic, occasionally ecstatic
And my baggy shorts crackle with bri-nylon static
But I'll pick up a drop shot noting a sweet spot
And foot fault a rough draft for smashing an ink blot
Through three sixty vistas in green flash blisters
With a code violation for spitting tongue twisters

It's an unusual approach but don't forget
If you struggle with your words you can just play a let
'cos I'm a no-holds bard, authentic wild card
A real hit 'em early, make it count die-hard

Air shots, deflections, the top edge over the wall
The stumble and tumble - I've mastered them all
So while you're waiting for your balls
To rebound off the firmament
Remember form is temporary
Class is permanent

If Only

Wimbledon – A note to Andy Murray

If you can keep your head
When all about you
Hold great expectations
In red, white and blue
If you can trust yourself
When others doubt you
For having dandruff
While you endorse shampoo
If you can serve up an ace
While cooking on grass
Turn the back-handed compliment
Into a pass

If you can ignore the roar
And the stifled cough
Even though you're moving
Like your strawberries have gone off
If you can match the big service
And nail it down the line
Lob in a bit of magic
Barley water into wine
If you can hold your nerve
And keep your dreams alive
Maybe win in three sets
And not hold out for five
If you can dispense with the need
For the weaker second serve
And crank up the desire
The vigour and the verve
If you can fill every minute
With sixty seconds of steel
And scatter the seeds of discontent
While keeping it real

If you can force your heart
To rule your head
And dangle your trainers
Where others fear to tread
If you can keep that mental strength intact
And not go round the bend
You'll be more than just a winner
You'll be a miracle. The end

Ball Game

Wimbledon - The boys and girls with the balls

A ball's width from the stroke of midday
All finely tuned, uniform and proud
The first shift of the day clocks on
Unnoticed by most of the crowd

Wrapped in a calm exterior
The Nike sole of discretion
Side by side with the good and the great
Now the court's once more in session

Well-rehearsed hands
Crack a six pack
And effortlessly
Pour out ammunition
It's a tricky little number
At the best of times
And why lesser mortals
Fail the audition

They are the cream
Without the strawberries
They are the chosen few
Without them in the chorus line
It would all fall apart
They hold it all together like superglue

With their rhythmic cameos
By accident and design
Lining up the passing shots
Straight back down the line
Shape-shifting, scene stealing
The cheeky pass and move
All meticulously choreographed
In a finger-snapping groove

So ball boys and ball girls
Take your curtain call
You Cinderellas and Cinderfellas
Will always go to the ball

When Rain Reigns

Wimbledon Rain - The other certainty after death and taxes

It's advantage no-one when rain reigns
And the great bath in the sky is up-ended
The umpire climbs down from his high chair
And the tannoy calls 'play is suspended'

And it's never that well-mannered fine rain
The one that soaks you right through
It's always that corrupt and sadistic stuff
That could re-float the QE2

Spears, stair rods and javelins
Arrows, buckets and frogs
If this was the score in Tokyo
It'd be raining Datsun cogs

Cue the fantastic, elastic expanse of green plastic
Pulled by hardy perennial fellas
While the beamer, the dreamer and the odd blasphemer
Crawl under creative umbrellas

The Little Jack Horners who huddle in corners
Waiting to pull out a plumb
With that feeling you get when you sit on a seat
Still warm from some other bloke's bum

So the rain in the main tops up the champagne
Like rocket fuels salad dressing
But the worrying thing is if Cliff has to sing
That could be extremely distressing

So it's advantage no-one when rain reigns
And the great bath in the sky is up-ended
But when all said and done, just think of the fun
You'll have with the bag you've befriended

Backword

I think I first encountered Keith when I was cycling clockwise around the North Pole. A cyclist, wearing nothing but an especially-designed, cold-weather, thermal suit (made me look silly in my shorts and T-shirt) came cycling in an anti-clockwise direction towards me. He gave me a cheery wave … difficult as he was strumming a Welsh Harp … the way fellow cyclists do, such is the Code of the International Brotherhood of Cyclists.

Seven months, three weeks and two days later to the day, I was driving on the M53 towards Chester, determined to take advantage of the January sales (which turned out to be a mistake because it was August). The weather was atrocious; the rain was torrential. On the hard shoulder, coming towards me, was a man on a bicycle, wearing nothing but a jaunty yellow sou'wester (the rider, not the bike … that would have been silly).

The cyclist splashed passed, and as he did I glimpsed the face - and the face of the cyclist at the North Pole flashed across my memory. But before I could do a u-turn on the hard shoulder – illegal I know, but curiosity would have got the better of me – the cyclist was up the embankment, over the fence and disappearing into the ploughed distance. I decided to scratch my head and call it a day … it was a Sunday.

Then, when I met Keith, I thought … is that the face of the North Pole/M53 Cyclist? During a lull in a chat about poetry, I cleverly turned the conversation to cycling by dropping a doughnut to the floor, and asked if indeed it had been Keith strumming the Harp and cycling anti-clockwise around the North Pole and then cycling naked the wrong way on the M53.

He gave me a funny look … well, it made me laugh … and we went back to chatting about the consequences of bad poetry on the lymph glands.

Since that first meeting several moons ago, I have been actively exposed to Keith's words and music and every single time I have been startled by his talent and skill at writing, composing and performing … but I still reckon he was that cyclist.

John Gorman